DAVID JOHNSTON

On a singular book of Cervidius Scaevola

Freiburger Rechtsgeschichtliche Abhandlungen

Herausgegeben vom Institut für Rechtsgeschichte und
geschichtliche Rechtsvergleichung der Albert-Ludwigs-Universität, Freiburg i. Br.

Neue Folge · Band 10

On a singular book of Cervidius Scaevola

By

David Johnston

DUNCKER & HUMBLOT / BERLIN

Gedruckt mit Unterstützung
der Gerda Henkel Stiftung, Düsseldorf

CIP-Kurztitelaufnahme der Deutschen Bibliothek

Johnston, David:
On a singular book of Cervidius Scaevola / by
David Johnston. — Berlin : Duncker u. Humblot,
1987.
 (Freiburger rechtsgeschichtliche Abhandlungen ;
N. F., Bd. 10)
 ISBN 3-428-06292-2

NE: GT

Alle Rechte vorbehalten
© 1987 Duncker & Humblot GmbH, Berlin 41
Satz: Irma Grininger, Berlin 62
Druck: Berliner Buchdruckerei Union GmbH, Berlin 61
Printed in Germany
ISBN 3-428-06292-2

Preface

Nihil aeque in causis agendis ut brevitas placet. This essay is short, but longer all the same than the work on which it comments. How can this be justified? If at all, because it is not just an analysis of one work. It is also an attempt, using the detail of one work as a model, to draw broader conclusions about the activities and preoccupations of the post-classical law schools.

Roman legal history is largely about the interpretation of texts; much turns on the textual-critical position adopted towards them. The line taken in this essay may seem to many too radical. The 'Interpolationenjagd' of the twenties and thirties gave textual criticism a bad name, but now it is so far out of fashion that the texts are treated in a manner which is not just conservative but often wholly uncritical. Yet if the arguments of the following chapters are right, then it is clear that this approach is not good enough. It would be wrong to revert to hyper-criticism. But it is essential to recognise that in a society whose law is evolving the textual transmission of legal writings is highly complex. The changes wrought by Justinian's legislation are regularly acknowledged. But it is unjustifiable to ignore the extent to which texts may have been transformed by the more subtle editing of his post-classical predecessors. Even a singular work may show traces of a plurality of hands.

Almost all of this essay was written between September 1985 and March 1986 during a visit to the Institut für Rechtsgeschichte und geschichtliche Rechtsvergleichung of the University of Freiburg. I have three main debts to acknowledge: first, to Professor Joseph Georg Wolf for inviting me to Freiburg, for generous help and hospitality, and for valuable discussion; second, to the Gerda Henkel Stiftung, not only for liberal support of my stay in Freiburg but also for a substantial contribution towards the publication costs; third, to the staff of the Institut and to the students who attended Professor Wolf's legal history seminar, in which many texts of Scaevola were examined.

In Freiburg I also had the benefit of discussing several points with Professor Detlef Liebs and particularly Karen Bauer. In London a sketch of the argument was presented to a seminar in the Faculty of Laws, University College: on the vigorous reaction of the participants, especially Professor Tony Honoré, followed much rethinking and (I hope) improvement. To all of these people I am grateful; agreement with my arguments is not to be presumed of any of them.

Christ's College, Cambridge D.E.L.J.
February 1987

Contents

I. Introduction	11
II. Analysis	14
1. Pal.186: D24.3.65	14
2. Pal.187pr: D28.6.48pr	14
3. Pal.187.1: D28.6.48.1	17
4. Pal.187.2: D28.6.48.2	30
5. Pal.188pr-1: D32.103pr-1	32
6. Pal.188.2-3: D32.103.2-3	37
7. Pal.189: D35.2.96	40
8. Pal.190: D36.1.81	43
9. Pal.191: D42.8.24	47
10. Pal.192: D44.3.14	60
11. Pal.193: D46.3.93	65
12. Pal.194: D46.7.21	70
III. Synthesis	79
1. Introduction	79
2. Six criteria	81
(a) Structure	81
(b) Sources	82
(c) Genre	84
(d) Location	85
(e) Content	87
(f) Language	87
3. Three hypotheses	91
(a) Epitome	91
(b) Substantial annotation	93
(c) Wholly spurious?	94
IV. Conclusions	97
Index of sources	101

Abbreviations and short titles

ANRW	Aufstieg und Niedergang der römischen Welt (ed. H. Temporini)
BIDR	Bullettino dell'istituto di diritto romano
CDJ	Concordance to the Digest Jurists (ed. T. Honoré and J. Menner)
LSQPT	*liber singularis quaestionum publice tractatarum*
Pal.	O. Lenel, Palingenesia iuris civilis (Leipzig, 1889)
RHD	Revue historique de droit francais et étranger
SDHI	Studia et documenta historiae et iuris
VIR	Vocabularium iurisprudentiae romanae
W. W. Buckland, Textbook	A textbook of Roman law^3, revised by Peter Stein (Cambridge, 1963)
M. Kaser, RP	Das römische Privatrecht^2 I (1971) II (1975) (Munich)
M. Kaser, RZ	Das römische Zivilprozessrecht (Munich, 1966)
P. Krueger, Geschichte	Geschichte der Quellen und Literatur des römischen Rechts^2 (Munich-Leipzig, 1912)
F. Schulz, Geschichte	Geschichte der römischen Rechtswissenschaft (Weimar, 1961)
F. Schulz, History	History of Roman legal science (Oxford, 1946)

Other abbreviations may be found at the beginning of *Kaser* RP I.

I. Introduction

Nine fragments of Scaevola's *liber singularis quaestionum publice tractatarum* are preserved in the Digest. This is an attempt to draw from them some conclusions about the original contents and character of the book, about its passage through post-classical times and the hands of the compilers.

Verdicts on the book have already been pronounced, unfavourably. *Beseler:* 'Diese Schrift ist ein nachklassischer paraphrastisch erweiterter Auszug aus Scaevolas Quästionen, zu denen sie sich ähnlich verhält wie der Gaius von Autun zu Gaius'[1]. *Schulz* in 1935: 'Insbes. wird zu prüfen sein, ob nicht, wenn von demselben Autor über dieselbe Materie ein liber singularis und ein mehrere Bücher umfassendes Werk vorliegt, der liber singularis eine nachklassische Epitome ist'[2]. But ten years or so later he abandoned such circumspection: 'A work known only from a few extracts in the Digest; these seem to come from a post-classical epitome, the author of which has added remarks of his own. They certainly contain considerable post-classical, pre-Justinian, work'[3].

The disadvantage of these verdicts is that they are based on evidence which is not recounted (*Schulz*) or which is presented in lapidary and laconic form (*Beseler*). The verdict reached at the end of this study will offer at least one advantage: that it is based on conclusions drawn expressly from an examination of the form, language and content of the LSQPT.

Difficulties begin with the title, which is unique. Legal and literary works fail to offer a compelling parallel. Writers who were not content to call their works simply *quaestiones* mostly opted either for a more illuminating title (*quaestiones naturales*[4]) or for a less prosaic one (*quaestiones epistolicae*[5]; *quaestiones Plautinae*[6]; or, more intriguing still, *quaestiones confusae*[7]). Scaevola's title however falls neither into one of the familiar moulds nor among the exotica[8]: the

---

[1] SZ 44 (1924) 359.

[2] 'Überlieferungsgeschichte der *responsa* des Cervidius Scaevola', Symbolae Lenel (Leipzig, 1935) 226n2.

[3] History 233 (= Geschichte 295).

[4] Seneca; Apuleius *Apologia* 36.

[5] Varro: Gellius NA 14.8.2; Cato: Gellius 6.10.2 (although Lipsius emends *Catonis* to *Varronis*).

[6] Varro.

[7] Julius Modestus (Gellius NA 3.9.1); cf. RE X.680- (1917) s.v. Julius 363 (Tolkiehn).

[8] For some good examples, Gellius NA *praefatio* 5-9. Among juristic works it is sufficient to refer to the *libri membranarum* of Neratius Priscus and the *libri coniectaneorum* of Alfenus Varus (cited by Gellius NA 7.5.1).

description *quaestiones publice tractatae* is neither illuminating nor very inspiring. Before what public were the questions treated[9]? Whether the title reflects a peculiarity of content or form is a problem which must wait until the individual texts have been discussed[10].

That the work is a *liber singularis* offers further difficulty. They are rare until the Severan period[11], before which the only writer who produced more than one is Gaius. Further, they generally have specific themes, especially in the area of administrative or public law. Often they take the form of commentaries on individual *senatusconsulta*. Their purposes are practical[12]. Yet a *liber singularis quaestionum* is a mixture of two genres, of practical monograph and problematic work. It is worth mentioning briefly the very few other works for which the same can be said. It is not possible here to discuss them fully or draw conclusions as to their authenticity.

(1) Julian *liber singularis de ambiguitatibus*. While the work has been thought to be a post-classical abridgement of Julian's *digesta*, more recent studies argue in favour of its classicality[13]. There is no doubt that the title is well-suited to the contents, which are concerned exclusively with verbal ambiguity, some of it admittedly not very perplexing.

(2) Gaius *liber singularis de casibus*. The subject matter is diverse, largely problematic, but not invariably of great interest[14].

(3) Modestinus *liber singularis de enucleatis casibus*. In spite of its title, the work does not appear to have a problematic character: the surviving fragments are concerned largely with public law. The private-law problems are neither of great difficulty nor of particular interest. It seems necessary to conclude with Schulz that the work makes 'an unfavourable impression' and may be postclassical[15].

---

[9] Is there a link with public *disputatio*? Cf. C9.41.11.1 (AD 290) *Domitius Ulpianus in publicarum disputationum libris*.

[10] Cf. the suggestion of *Beseler*, Beiträge III 160 on Pal. 187.1 'Oder hat Sc das Stenogramm seines Vortrages drucken lassen?'

[11] This formulation is to be preferred to that of *Schulz*, History 257 (= Geschichte 330) that 'classical jurisprudence produced hardly any monographs'. Cf. the strictures of *F. Wieacker*, Textstufen 60n13 (61).

[12] *Wieacker*, Textstufen 389-.

[13] *Schulz*, History 230 (= Geschichte 291); contra *J. Miquel*, SZ 87 (1970) 103- on D34.5.13.2- cf. *A. Torrent*, Salvius Julianus liber singularis de ambiguitatibus (Salamanca, 1971) but with the unenviable review of *F. Horak*, SZ 90 (1973) 411-421.

[14] *D. Liebs*, ANRW II.15 (1976) 338 describes it as a 'Sammlung von eher sonderbaren als praktischen Fällen'.

[15] *Schulz*, History 242 (= Geschichte 308).

(4) Modestinus *liber singularis de heurematicis*. Most of this is problematic, some of it rather recherché (like its title whose origin and significance remain obscure[16]). Some of it has the character of giving practical advice[17].

Intructions should raise but not prejudge problems. This one has limited itself to pointing out that the origin and purpose of the LSQPT are unclear; its title unusual and uninformative; the genre a hybrid and the format rare. This may raise doubts (and some have had them), but a balanced judgement requires more evidence. Chapter II examines each surviving text of the work in detail. The third chapter draws this detailed evidence together with more general reflections, and the fourth pronounces a verdict.

---

[16] *Schulz*, ibid. But a work εὑρημάτων is mentioned by Gellius NA *praefatio* 6.
[17] Especially Pal. 73 and 79.

II. Analysis

1. Pal.186: D24.3.65[1]

Haec actio etiam constante matrimonio mulieri competit.

Not much need be said about this fragment. It refers to an action based on the *lex Iulia de maritandis ordinibus*, as was already recognised by *Cujas*[2]. A text of Paul makes clear that the action was based on a *lex Iulia*[3]; and D24.3.64, the fragment preceding this one, shows which *lex Iulia*: since the fragment is from book 7 of Ulpian's *libri ad legem Iuliam et Papiam*, it reduces the possible *leges Iuliae* to only one, the *lex Iulia de maritandis ordinibus*[4]. Ulpian's fragment discusses various details of the cases in which the action was available and for what amounts it lay. In D24.3.64.10 (the text immediately preceding this fragment of Scaevola), Ulpian is concerned with the action which lay to the wife against her husband and his heirs for any money they had obtained from selling a dotal slave. The details are not important here[5].

Scaevola makes only one point here, that the action is available to the wife even during the course of the marriage. This is however a crucial point, since it at once distinguishes this action from the *actio rei uxoriae* which by its nature is available only after dissolution of the marriage[6].

2. Pal.187pr: D28.6.48pr[7]

Servum communem habemus: hic heres scriptus est et, si heres non sit, Maevius illi substitutus est: alterius iussu dominorum adiit hereditatem, alterius non: quaeritur an substituto locus sit an non. et verius est substituto locum esse.

---

[1] Translation: This action is available to a woman even during her marriage.

[2] *Observationes* 2.34.

[3] Paul D48.10.14.2.

[4] This is generally recognised: cf. R. *Astolfi*, La lex Iulia et Papia (Padua, 1970) 72-. But *A. Söllner*, Zur Vorgeschichte und Funktion der *actio rei uxoriae* (Köln-Wien, 1969) 37 seems misleadingly to suggest that this prohibition, like that on unauthorised alienation of dotal land, was contained in the *lex Iulia de adulteriis*.

[5] *Astolfi*, loc. cit.

[6] Cf. *Kaser*, RP I 334 who recognises this therefore as a 'besondere Klage'.

[7] Translation: We own a slave jointly. He has been instituted heir, and Maevius substituted to him for the event that he does not become heir. On the instructions of one of his owners, but not of the other, he has accepted the inheritance. The question is whether the substitute has a place or not. And it is more correct to say that he has.

What happens if A, one of the owners of a slave, gives him the *iussum* to enter an estate to which he has been instituted heir but B, the other owner, does not? Ulpian's *regulae* have an answer[8]:

> Ulp. D29.2.67 lib 1 regularum[9]. Servus communis ab extero heres institutus si iussu unius adierit hereditatem, non pro maiore parte interim heredem eum facit quam pro dominica, deinde ceteris sociis non iubentibus tacito iure partes ei adcrescunt.

For the time being the slave acquires for A, the owner who gives the *iussum*, in proportion to his share in him[10]. But what if the slave has a substitute? Ulpian does not discuss the matter, but Scaevola's problem is to decide between two possible solutions. The first is that B's share should accrue to that of A. A would obtain the whole, and the substitute would be excluded. The second is that the substitute should be admitted to the share not taken up by B. Scaevola opts for giving preference to the substitute.

No clauses are quoted from the will, so it must be assumed that the interpretation given by Scaevola relates to an ordinary institution and substitution rather than to any special form. The will would have read: *Stichus heres esto. si Stichus heres non erit, Maevius heres esto.* So the condition to which the substitution is subject is that Stichus should not be heir. But we are specifically told that the slave has made *aditio*. Therefore the institution has not failed, and there can be no place for the substitution.

Literal interpretation of the will demands rejection of Maevius' claim. But Scaevola's solution is the opposite: he admits the substitute and so plainly rules out accrual of the second share to the first[11]. The justification of this solution can be found only in the conception of common ownership which Scaevola is employing. A common slave could be regarded in effect as two slaves, his institution as two independent institutions. An example of this conception is found in relation to a legacy *per vindicationem* in Julian:

> Jul. D30.81.1 lib 32 digestorum[12]. Si servo communi res legata fuisset, potest alter dominus agnoscere legatum, alter repellere: nam in hanc causam servus communis quasi duo servi sunt.

---

[8] There is good reason to think Ulpian's *regulae* spurious: see *T. Honoré, Ulpian* (Oxford, 1982) 107-113. But there is no reason why the legal argument produced in this text should not have been espoused by a classical jurist.

[9] Translation: If a common slave instituted heir by a third party has, on the instructions of one of his owners, accepted an inheritance, he does not in the meantime make that owner heir for a greater share than he owns in the slave. But subsequently, as other co-owners fail to give him instructions to accept, their shares tacitly accrue to that owner.

[10] Some details of the *aditio* remain obscure: within what time it must be made is not stated, but the limit for *cretio* would be the most obvious terminus (G2.174); some declaration must presumably have been made by the slave on whose behalf he was making *aditio*. That is clearly presupposed by this text, and indicated by Paul D29.2.68 lib 5 ad legem Iuliam et Papiam which envisages multiple *aditiones* on behalf of individual *domini*.

[11] Unless of course the substitute were to refuse: cf. Ulp. D37.11.2.8 lib 41 ad edictum.

No generalisation is made: Julian specifically limits his point to this case[13]. Yet the most obvious path by which Scaevola could have come to the solution he propounds is precisely the same. If the common slave is regarded as two slaves then his institution can be regarded as two institutions, first *qua* slave of A, then *qua* slave of B. Then it can be argued that entry only *qua* slave of A satisfies the condition *si Stichus heres non erit*, since Stichus has not entered *qua* slave of B. The substitute can therefore be admitted[14].

This version may appear somewhat far-fetched. That is on the presumption that one regards the 'double slave' conception of the common slave as implausible, as well one might. But for a jurist who had adopted it, the construction just outlined would appear compelling. The matter is therefore ultimately reduced to conceptions of common ownership, into which we shall go no further. The words *et verius est* indicate that there was controversy, details of which may have been eliminated by Justinian. But on which side of the fence should we expect to find Scaevola? *Bretone* argues that Scaevola would not have adhered to the theory of the 'doppia persona', which he believes to be a Sabinian one; rather, to judge from other texts, Scaevola would have followed a rigorous Proculian line and excluded the substitute[15].

Similarly *Cosentini* argued that Scaevola must have reached the opposite conclusion in this text and preferred accrual to the substitution; the compilers have amended his view and from *et verius est* the text no longer reproduces Scaevola[16]. He cites the following in support[17]:

Iav. D29.2.64 lib 2 ex posterioribus Labeonis. Servus duorum heres institutus *et adire iussus si alterius domini iussu adierit, deinde manumissus fuerit, poterit ipse adeundo ex parte dimidia heres esse,
*et adire iussus *del. Mo.*

---

[12] Translation: If something has been left by legacy to a jointly-owned slave, one owner can accept it and the other reject it: for in this case a jointly-owned slave is like two slaves.

[13] So far as the legacy is concerned, it is worth noting that this decision does not run along school lines: Cels. D31.20 lib 19 digestorum makes plain that the Proculians took the same view. It is true of course that the same considerations do not apply to a legacy to a slave as do to an estate (Scaevola's case), for which an heir must be found to the whole, but it is in both cases the conception of the common slave as two slaves which rules out accrual.

[14] It is not a matter of the common slave's having two substitutes: the substitute is regarded as substituted for the share not already acquired, that is for the share of the co-owner who fails to give the *iussum*.

[15] M. Bretone, Servus communis (Naples, 1958) 114n26 etc. His view that Scaevola cannot have reached this decision depends on Scaev. D45.3.19 and citations of Scaevola in Ulp. D41.1.23.3 and D7.1.25.6. But all these texts appear to have been altered, so caution is required in deriving from them a conclusion to apply to D28.6.48pr. However that may be, there was evidently a classical controversy (*Bretone* 114-6), so that the main amendment we need suppose is the elimination of the details of it in the course of the compilation.

[16] C. Cosentini, IURA 1 (1950) 275-280.

[17] Translations: A slave owned by two owners was instituted heir. If he accepted the inheritance on the instructions of one owner and has then been freed, by accepting the

Paul D29.2.65 lib 2 ad Sabinum. et si substitutum haberet idem servus ita 'si heres non erit, ille heres esto' substitutus locum non habet.

The substitute is excluded. But to base a counter-argument on such a textual chain is dangerous, since it is unclear on what original premises Paul's solution may have been based. We cannot simply suppose as *Cosentini* does that they would have been the same as in Scaevola's case. There is also no need, even if Paul was discussing the same problem, to suppose that he would have reached the same solution as Scaevola. Even if the matter was viewed on school lines (which is itself less than plain), the status of the schools in the late-classical period is uncertain, and if Paul is to be associated on the whole with the Proculians, there is not much evidence for Scaevola[18].

3. Pal.187.1: D28.6.48.1 [19]

'Titius heres esto. Stichum Maevio do lego. Stichus heres esto. si Stichus heres non erit, Stichus liber heresque esto.' in hac quaestione in primis quaerendum est utrum unus gradus sit an duo et an causa mutata sit substitutionis an eadem permaneat. et quidem in plerisque quaeritur an ipse sibi substitui possit et respondetur causa institutionis mutata substitui posse. igitur si Titius heres scriptus sit et, si heres non sit, idem heres

---

inheritance himself he will be able to be heir to a half share ... and if he has a substitute on the following terms 'if he should not be heir, let that man be heir' the substitute has no place.

[18] D. Liebs, ANRW II.15 (1976) 283-4. Scaevola rarely takes sides, but when he does so in fact joins the Sabinians twice (no. 39 and no. 55 in *Liebs'* checklist of controversies) and the Proculians once (no. 25). As for Scaevola's methods of argumentation, *Honoré* TR 32 (1964) 8 says that a 'percentage of rationality' below 50 is generally an indication of a Proculian pen. Scaevola scores 46, but this seems to me to be too close to the borderline to be decisive.

[19] Translation: 'Let Titius be heir. I give and bequeath Stichus to Maevius. Let Stichus be heir. If Stichus should not be heir, let Stichus be free and heir.' In this problem the first question is whether there is one grade or two, and whether the *causa* of the substitution is changed or remains the same. And certainly in several cases it is asked whether someone can be substituted to himself and the answer is given that he can be if the *causa* of the institution is changed. Therefore if Titius is instituted heir and, if he does not become heir, himself instructed to be heir, the substitution will be of no force. But if someone is instituted heir conditionally but substituted unconditionally, the *causa* does change, since the condition on the institution can fail and the substitution can therefore be of some use. But if the condition has been satisfied, both <dispositions> are unconditional and therefore the substitution will be of no force. On the other hand if someone is instituted unconditionally and substituted to himself conditionally, the conditional substitution is ineffective and <the *causa*> is not understood to have changed, since even if the condition is satisfied there will be two unconditional institutions. On these principles the problem is made clear: 'Let Titius be heir. I give and bequeath Stichus to Maevius. Let Stichus be heir. If Stichus should not be heir, let Stichus be free and heir.' We have learned that, since in the same will Stichus is both legated and has received his freedom, freedom prevails, and if freedom prevails the legacy is not due, and therefore Stichus cannot accept the inheritance on the instructions of the legatee, and for this reason it is true that he is not heir, and from the subsequent words he obtains his freedom: since there is evidently one grade. But what if Titius does not enter? On the basis of the substitution Stichus will become free and heir. For, as long as he does not accept on the instructions of the legatee, he is not regarded as having become the property of the legatee on account of the legacy, and so it is certain that he is not heir, and for this reason from the words 'if he should not be heir, let Stichus be free and heir' he will become free and heir. In his work Julian also approves our view.

iussus sit, substitutio nullius momenti erit. sed si sub condicione quis heres scriptus sit, pure autem substitutus est, causa immutatur quoniam potest ex institutione defici condicio et substitutio aliquid adferre: sed si exstiterit condicio, duae purae sunt et ideo nullius momenti erit substitutio. contra si pure quis instituatur, deinde sub condicione sibi substituatur, nihil facit substitutio condicionalis nec mutata intellegatur, quippe cum et si exstiterit condicio duae purae sunt institutiones. secundum haec proposita quaestio manifestetur: 'Titius heres esto. Stichum Maevio do lego. Stichus heres esto. si Stichus heres non erit, Stichus liber heresque esto.' nos didicimus quoniam eodem testamento et legatus sit Stichus et libertatem accepit praevalere libertatem et, si praevalet libertas, non deberi legatum et ideo iussu legatarii non posse adire hereditatem, ac per hoc verum esse Stichum heredem non esse et ex sequentibus verbis libertatem illi competere: cum unus gradus videtur. quid ergo si non adierit Titius? incipiet substitutione Stichus liber et heres esse. porro quamdiu non adit iussu legatarii nec ex causa legati intellegitur legatarii esse effectus et ideo certum est illum heredem non esse, ac per hoc ex his verbis 'si heres non erit, Stichus liber heresque esto' liber et heres existet. hoc autem quod sentimus Iulianus quoque in libris suis probat.

I

The text presents a long not always lucid discussion of provisions quoted from a will real or imaginary. The situation is as follows: the testator has instituted an heir, Titius; legated his slave Stichus *per vindicationem* to Maevius; instituted Stichus heir; and substituted for the case that Stichus should not become heir Stichus with freedom. The provisions are complex[20], but the most likely intention of the testator is no doubt that Titius should become heir and Maevius acquire the legacy; that Maevius should then instruct his newly-acquired slave Stichus to enter the estate and so through him obtain (say) half the estate. If Maevius fails to give the *iussum,* Stichus fails to become heir and then through the substitution becomes free and heir in his own right. The result is that if the first grade of the will (institution) operates the estate will be shared by Titius and Maevius; if the second (substitution) by Titius and Stichus.

Yet there are problems. (1) Is the institution of Stichus *sine libertate* valid? Normally of course the institution of one's own slave without freedom is void[21], but the question arises whether it might somehow be redeemed here by the prior legacy to Maevius. (2) Is the institution of Stichus problematic on another ground, that he belonged to the testator at the time of testation and death but not at the time the institution was due to operate? (3) Is the legacy valid or vitiated by the fact that it is written in the will before the substitution[22]? (4) Is the sub-

---

[20] It is perhaps worth noting that the Basilica (35.10.45) appear to assume that such a will could only have come into being as a consequence of gradual addition of clauses, resulting in chaos: before the institution of the slave they read εἶτα παρακατιών. Some modern views are equally despairing: *Buckland,* Slavery 510; *C. Tumedei,* Rivista italiana per le scienze giuridiche 63 (1919) 67-108 at 80-85.

[21] G2.185-8; UE 22.12. The contrary view of Atilicinus was not adopted until Justinian: Inst. 2.14pr.

[22] *Voci* DER II 580n53.

stitution effective? Or invalid owing to the lack of a change of *causa*? And if invalid, will Stichus become either free or heir or both[23]?

It is remarkable that only the last of these difficulties is considered in the text. For only one of them can be disposed of without difficulty: the legacy appears to be valid. As required for a legacy *per vindicationem* the object is the property of the testator both at the time of testation and of death[24]. That it precedes the substitution does not seem problematic, since legacies are charged on the heir whose name they follow[25]. The legacy of Stichus is therefore charged on Titius and fails only if he does not enter (or if Maevius does not accept it[26]). It is in any case impossible to consider charging the legacy of Stichus on Stichus, so that while it is true to say that if Stichus becomes heir on the basis of the substitution the legacy will fail, the truth of this proposition depends not on formal grounds but on practical ones[27].

Problems (1) and (2) are of course related; in fact on the basis of a text of Gaius, (2) can be subsumed under (1)[28]:

G2.187. nam si sine libertate heres institutus sit, etiamsi postea manumissus fuerit a domino, heres esse non potest, quia institutio in persona eius non constitit; ideoque licet alienatus sit non potest iussu domini novi cernere hereditatem.

This text makes plain that institution by a testator of his own slave without freedom is *ab initio* void and that it cannot, in spite of subsequent alienation of the slave, have any force[29]. Quite simply, after alienation the slave is regarded as a different person; different from the one instituted. So far as we can judge from Gaius, at classical law it is the *persona* of the slave at the time of testation, together with the rules on validity which that brings with it, which is relevant. The second problem therefore is reduced to the first: whether in any circumstances the institution of one's own slave *sine libertate* can be valid.

---

[23] G. v. Beseler, SZ66 (1948) 314n26; W. W. Buckland, The Roman law of slavery (Cambridge, 1908) 469; *Mommsen* ed. maior ad loc.

[24] G2.196.

[25] *Voci*, DER II 169n34.

[26] G2.195: the Proculian view that for a legacy *per vindicationem* an initial acceptance by the legatee was required prevailed over the Sabinian view that it was acquired automatically and had then to be expressly rejected if so desired by the legatee.

[27] It is worth noting here that (on the hypothesis that institution and substitution are also valid) the legacy is under a resolutive condition of giving the *iussum*: if Maevius fails to instruct Stichus to enter then he loses the legacy, as Stichus will become free and heir under the substitution. Maevius must choose therefore between having Stichus plus a share of the estate and having nothing at all.

[28] Translation: For if he has been instituted heir without freedom, even if he has later been freed by his owner, he cannot be heir because the institution does not exist in his person; and so although he has been sold he cannot accept the inheritance on the instructions of his new owner.

[29] One might have argued that, since it was in effect institution of a *servus alienus*, institution *sine libertate* was in fact the correct form, and that institution *cum libertate* would have been void: Flor. D28.5.50pr lib 10 institutionum; cf. PS 3.4b.7.

On this point however the texts are not very forthcoming: they stress only the absolute invalidity of such an institution and whether it might conceivably be validated by a preceding legacy is a problem found not at all in the sources. Justinian indicates that views differed[30]:

> C6.27.5. (531). Quidam cum testamentum conderet duobus heredibus scriptis unum quidem ex parte instituit, servum autem suum cuius et nomen addidit ex reliqua parte sine libertate scripsit heredem, et postea eundem servum alii legavit vel post institutionem heredis servum per legatum alii adsignavit, et tunc heredem eum sine libertate instituit: et dubitabatur si huiusmodi legatum vel institutio aliquas vires potest habere et cui adquiritur legatum vel institutio. (1) Dubitationis autem materia erat quod adhuc servum suum constitutum heredem sine libertate scripserat, et tanta inter veteres exorta est contentio ut vix possibile sit videri eandem decidere. (1a) ...

Justinian goes on to dispose of the problem by decreeing that an institution shall imply a gift of liberty. So, an end to *materia dubitationis*. Yet for the classics the two poles of argument seem clear: a strict view refusing to depart from the principle of invalidity of institution *sine libertate;* a hardly less strict but opposed view that institution *sine libertate* was in fact the correct form if a legacy preceded. It is true that on this view there would be a need to regard the institution as in some way suspended until the legacy had been acquired[31].

Scaevola's view scarcely emerges from this text, for it is not this question at all but another which is said to be fundamental. That is the issue whether there is one *gradus* or two. The point of this question is best understood from a text of Ulpian.

II

> Ulp. D28.6.10.7 lib 4 ad Sabinum[32]. Nemo institutus et sibi substitutus sine causae mutatione quicquam proficit, sed hoc in uno gradu: ceterum si duo sint gradus potest dici valere substitutionem ut Iulianus libro trigesimo digestorum putat: si quidem sic sit substitutus sibi cum haberet coheredem Titium 'si Stichus heres non erit, liber et heres esto' non valere substitutionem. quod si ita: 'si Titius heres non erit, tunc Stichus liber et

---

[30] Translation: A certain person when making a will instituted two heirs, one to a share, but to the remainder he instituted his own slave (whose name he added) without giving him his freedom, and later left the slave by legacy to a third person. Or after the institution of the heir he gave the slave to the third person by legacy, and then instituted him heir without giving him his freedom. The problem was whether a legacy or institution of this sort can have any force, and who benefits from them. (1) Yet the reason for the doubt was that the testator had instituted as heir without freedom someone who was still his own slave, and so much contention arose among the early jurists that it may seem scarcely possible to resolve it.

[31] *Buckland,* Slavery 468n4.

[32] Translation: Nobody gains anything from being instituted and substituted to himself without a change of *causa,* but this is one grade: but if there are two grades, it can be said that the substitution is valid, as Julian thinks in book 30 of his *digesta*: if somebody is substituted to himself when he has a co-heir, Titius, in this way 'if Stichus should not become heir, let him be free and heir', the substitution is invalid. But if it is like this 'if Titius should not become heir, then let Stichus be free and heir also to his share', then there are two grades and therefore if Titius refuses then Stichus will be free and heir.

heres et in eius partem esto' duos gradus esse atque ideo repudiante Titio Stichum liberum et heredem fore.

The text is not entirely clear as to the relations between *causa* and *gradus*. As for the terminology: *gradus* is normal usage for a 'degree' of institution: so the person who is the first choice as heir can be described as *primo gradu scriptus*, while someone substituted to him for the event that he does not accept the inheritance is *secundo gradu scriptus*; and someone substituted to the substitute would be *tertio gradu*[33]. So the institution of an heir is one *gradus*, and each level of substitution amounts to another. The text indicates that a *causa* somehow determines whether there is one or more *gradus*. What it states is (1) that there is no benefit to be had from being substituted to oneself without a change of *causa*, but (2) that if there are two *gradus* the substitution can be said to be valid[34]. The examples are intended to illuminate this statement. They both involve the institution of a slave, and both unfortunately fail to make it clear whether the slave is instituted with or without freedom. The examples must therefore be considered for both instances.

1. Here the will must read either:
   (a) Titius heres esto. Stichus heres esto.
       Si Stichus heres non erit, liber et heres esto.
or
   (b) Titius heres esto. Stichus liber et heres esto.
       Si Stichus heres non erit, liber et heres esto.

The substitution is stated to be invalid. Why? If (a) is correct, then the institution of Stichus is invalid, since it is *sine libertate*. Therefore Stichus will not become heir, and the substitution will necessarily take effect[35]. But to say in this case that the substitution is invalid is odd. If (b) is correct, then the institution of Stichus is valid. That this version is correct is supported by the problems with (a) and by the words *cum haberet coheredem Titium*[36], which are curious if the institution of Stichus is actually invalid. So if version (b) is right and the institution is valid, then Julian's point is that the substitution is invalid, apparently because there is no change of *causa:* Stichus is substituted under the same terms as he is instituted: in either case he will end up as coheir of Titius, so the only change is that he is to enter on substitution only if he has not done so on institution. Although there appear to be two *gradus*, of institution and substitution, in fact owing to the lack of a substantial difference (*causae mutatio*) between them there is really only one.

---

[33] See G2.174, 176; Ulp. D37.11.2.4 lib 41 ad edictum.

[34] The expression is rather lax, since if the substitution is valid there are *ipso facto* two *gradus*. But there does not seem to be any other way of understanding the text.

[35] So in this sense one could say that, as the substitution necessarily takes force at once, it amounts to being in the first *gradus*; and so this is a case of only one *gradus*. But the explanation given in the text seems more convincing.

[36] The subjunctive *haberet* depends only on the *oratio obliqua*.

The point seems banal. Yet in the context of a broader discussion of conditions on institution and substitution, it may have some value: it indicates that the words *si Stichus heres non erit* are not regarded as a valid condition on a substitution, if (as here) the satisfaction of the condition lies solely in Stichus' power. Various consequences flow from regarding dispositions as conditional or unconditional; Julian's point is perhaps just that for those purposes, this is not a real condition.

2. Again two versions of the will are required:
   (a) Titius heres esto. Stichus heres esto.
       Si Titius heres non erit, tunc Stichus liber et heres et in eius partem esto.
or
   (b) Titius heres esto. Stichus liber et heres esto.
       Si Titius heres non erit, tunc Stichus liber et heres et in eius partem esto.

Here there are said to be two *gradus* (the institution of Stichus and Titius, presumably, and the substitution), and the consequence is drawn that if Titius fails to accept the estate Stichus will be free and heir. This makes it sound rather as if Stichus only has a chance to be heir if Titius refuses, which would suggest that the institution is invalid and support version (a); but it may well be simply that the text is reporting the terms of the substitution in other words (*repudiante Titio* corresponds to the protasis of the substitution clause, and *Stichum liberum et heredem fore* to the apodosis), which takes us no further. In favour of version (b) are the words *et in eius partem,* which presuppose that Stichus has already been able to acquire his own share on institution[37]. Two other points support version (b): firstly, that the first example in the text seems to deal with a valid institution, so it is more natural to suppose that the second will do the same; secondly, that if in either example the institution is *sine libertate* and so void, no problem of conflict with the substitution can arise at all. The issue of distinguishing *gradus* by examining *causa* is pointless if one of the *gradus* is void *ab initio.*

There are two *gradus* because there is a meaningful condition separating institution and substitution: it does not lie in Stichus' power to determine whether the condition is satisfied and whether as a consequence he obtains the other share of the inheritance. A further difference between the substitution and the institution is that under the first Stichus becomes only coheir with Titius, whereas in the second he becomes sole heir. All the same, it is worth noting that the substitution is completely unnecessary, since if one coheir accepts an inheritance and the other declines, the second share accrues automatically to the first[38].

---

[37] It is true that these words are quoted from the will and so need not reflect strict legal reasoning, but just the assumptions of a testator. On the other hand this looks very like a hypothetical problem, in which precise use of language might be expected.

[38] See the cases cited in note 112.

If these arguments are correct, then Julian is concerned not with the problems of institution *sine libertate* but with how to differentiate *gradus*. A change of *causa* is required, and that amounts to ensuring that if there is the same beneficiary in each of two *gradus* he is a beneficiary on different terms in each one. That is what distinguishes Julian's two examples.

This however is not Scaevola's case. The provisions certainly read like those in Ulpian-Julian, but the legacy makes a crucial difference. If the legacy and institution *sine libertate* of Stichus are taken to be valid then the entry of Stichus is determined in the first grade wholly by other persons: Titius, who must enter; Maevius, who must accept the legacy and give the *iussum*. In the substitution on the other hand Stichus is himself appointed heir and freed. Here the substitution is by no means pointless; the question whether there is a material change of *causa* and therefore two *gradus* is much less clear.

Scaevola's discussion in this text falls into two parts, separated by the remarkable repetition of the clauses quoted from the will. General points comprise the first part in which *causa* and *gradus* are discussed; the second part gives closer attention to the interpretation of the will itself.

To begin at the beginning. The first of Scaevola's general examples resembles the first in Ulpian-Julian (*si Titius heres scriptus sit et, si heres non sit, idem heres iussus sit*). But from there on the discussions diverge. Scaevola's remaining two examples are these: (a) conditional institution and unconditional substitution: the *causa* changes so there are two *gradus*; (b) unconditional institution and conditional substitution: there is no change of *causa* and so only one *gradus*: the substitution is ineffective.

The reasoning: in the first case the substitution may be able to bring a benefit, but if the condition on the institution is realised the two dispositions are unconditional and the substitution is of no effect. This reasoning is not cogent. In the first place it is quite incorrect to describe a conditional disposition in which the condition has been satisfied as an unconditional disposition. Furthermore if the condition on an institution has been satisfied then the substitution is of no effect not because of some supposed lack of material difference between it and the institution, but precisely because a substitution is *anima naturaliter* intended to take effect only when the institution fails.

The reasoning is notably more abstract than in the text of Ulpian-Julian. There seems no doubt that this is a disadvantage, for the point clearly elaborated by Julian in relation to the provision '*si Titius heres non erit, tunc Stichus liber et heres et in eius partem esto*' is illuminated much less successfully by the formulation in terms of *sub condicione institutio* and *substitutio condicionalis*. For it is not difficult to think of conditions on an institution (such as *si Capitolium ascenderit* or—easier still—*non ascenderit*) which are so easily fulfilled, and which lie entirely in the power of the instituted heir, that if he should be substituted to himself it could be said literally, but not materially, that there was a change of *causa* and that there were therefore two *gradus*.

Yet the nature of the *causa/gradus* doctrine requires further consideration. Does it mean that the substitution is void *ab initio*? This is the only intelligible way of construing it, and this is the force the point appears to have in Julian's discussion. But in Scaevola the impression is given that the substitution is only void when, owing to the operation of the institution, it could no longer be of any possible value: *duae purae sunt et ideo nullius momenti erit substitutio*. But then the doctrine is wholly worthless, for any substitution is inoperative and of no force once the institution has operated. It is worth putting forward the hypothesis now that the whole of the discussion of *gradus* and *causa* in Scaevola is interpolated on the basis of a clumsy adaptation and elaboration of a point made by Julian in book 30 of his *digesta* and cited by Ulpian in his book 4 *ad Sabinum*.

Nonetheless it is no more than reasonable before dismissing the distinction to consider what possible arguments Scaevola could have extracted from it. This turns on the undecided point what his view on the institution *sine libertate* in this text was. (1) If he thought it invalid, there would be little point in considering *gradus*, since it would be most reasonable to consider the substitution as applying immediately in the case of an invalid institution[39]. (2) If he thought the institution valid, there would still be no point in raising the matter of *gradus*, provided that the institution of Stichus did in practice operate (this depends on the *iussum* of Maevius), for the substitution could be ignored. Only if the institution was valid but failed to operate does the question whether there is a change of *causa* become important[40].

Elimination seems to be the best treatment for the references to *causa* and *gradus* in this text. The consequences of the *causa* doctrine are not drawn; the doctrine seems unhelpful unless perhaps when applied in the manner of Julian; in the text of Scaevola it is neither clearly stated nor rationally applied.

---

[39] This consequence is not necessary, since it could be argued first that the substitution was invalid owing to the lack of a change of *causa*, and then that the institution was invalid owing to its being *sine libertate*. Yet on the whole I do not think this is likely to have been Scaevola's argument, even though *favor testamenti* would not stand against it, as it would lead only to accrual to the benefit of Titius.

[40] It might be thought from the text (and especially from the words *cum unus gradus videtur*) that this question also affects whether Stichus ends up free alone or free and also heir (cf. note 23). Yet the text is barely comprehensible at this point, and it seems unlikely that this is so: in the first argument it looks as if (owing to there being only one *gradus*) Stichus gains only his freedom when there is no *iussum legatarii*; but in the third argument (see below) it is specifically stated that if there is no *iussum* then Stichus acquires both freedom and the estate. This contradiction is a further pointer towards the interpolation of the *gradus* doctrine and its consequences.

III

Quite different arguments lead the text to its conclusions. There are three of these, produced in the second part of the text. This is the first. (1) 'We have learned that, where the same will makes a legacy of a slave and also gives him his freedom, freedom prevails.' This point is employed as the premise of the following argument: freedom prevails, therefore the legacy is not due; therefore the legatee cannot give the *iussum*; therefore Stichus cannot become heir; therefore Stichus becomes free under the substitution. The argument would be more convincing if its conclusion were not contained in its premise: it is a perfect *circulus in probando*. So much for the argument; what about the premise?

Other texts may be enlisted to see whether Scaevola could really have claimed that at his time lawyers had learned to give *libertas* priority where in a will it conflicted with a legacy.

> Marci. D40.5.50 lib 7 institutionum[41]. Si servus legatus et per fideicommissum manumissus sit, Cervidius Scaevola consultus putabat novissimam scripturam valere sive libertas sit sive legatum, quia cum libertatem datam postea placeat adimi, et per legatum constat posse adimi: sed si in obscuro sit qua mente post libertatem legavit eundem servum in obscuro libertatem praevalere. quae sententia mihi quoque verior esse videtur.

In this text Scaevola resolves the conflict between a legacy and a fideicommissary manumission by deciding that the later of the two dispositions is to be effective. To this is added the qualification that if the testator's intention in making the legacy subsequent to the *fideicommissum libertatis* is uncertain, then liberty should prevail. This qualification is odd[42]. Revocation of a gift of liberty is of course a serious matter for which a clear intention must be demanded. But the qualification completely fails to recognise that if the testator intended to make the legacy (and there is no argument to the effect that he did not) then it is clear that he no longer intended the slave to be freed.

We might have doubts about the text. *Beseler* for example thought the theory of *ademptio* of freedom through a legacy to be Justinianic[43], and states that in the struggle between *favor libertatis* and the testator's intentions Justinian gave the palm to the latter. Yet this doctrine is based entirely on assertions of interpolation in this text and the two cited immediately below[44]. Other scholars would

---

[41] Translation: If a slave has been legated and left his freedom by *fideicommissum*, on consultation Scaevola thought that the latest disposition should be valid whether it was the freedom or the legacy because, since it is agreed that a gift of freedom can be revoked, it is plain that it can also be revoked through a legacy. But if it should be unclear with what intention the testator made a legacy of the slave after the gift of freedom, then in uncertainty freedom is to prevail. This view also seems to me the better one.

[42] Cf. H. J. Wieling, Testamentsauslegung im römischen Recht (Munich, 1972) 113.

[43] *Beseler*, Beiträge II 103: [*sive libertas... praevalere*]; he also expunges *per fideicommissum*, but the differences between direct and fideicommissary manumission need not concern us here.

[44] *Harada*, SZ59 (1939) 502-5.

associate *favor libertatis* particularly with Justinian[45]. On examination of this text of Marcian, and of the two of Paul, what is most striking is that they fall into two parts, one favouring freedom, the other making cautious qualifications about the terms on which the legacy might instead prevail. There is great emphasis on evidentiary requirements, some of it hardly consistent (as we have seen in the text of Marcian) with the general principle enunciated. It is these evidentiary requirements which seem to me to be the most likely candidates to be interpolations[46]. All the same, for the texts of Paul, it is worth noting the point made by *Voci*[47] that if there appear to be two layers in the text the first may be attributable to Sabinus or to Vitellius, the second to Paul[48]:

> Paul D40.4.10.1 lib 4 ad Sabinum. Si servus legatus liber esse iussus est, liber est. sed si prius liber esse iussus postea legatus sit, si quidem evidens voluntas sit testatoris quod ademit libertatem, cum placeat hodie etiam libertatem adimi posse, legato eum cedere puto: quod si in obscuro sit tunc favorabilius respondetur liberum fore.
>
> Paul D31.14pr lib 4 ad Vitellium. Si idem servus et legatus et liber esse iussus sit, favor libertatis praevalet: sin autem et in posteriore scriptura legatus est et evidens ademptio libertatis ostenditur, legatum propter defuncti voluntatem praevalebit.

These texts give the general impression that to state, as is done in the text of Scaevola, that we have learned that liberty always takes precedence is to simplify and mislead. Rather, different texts provide varying solutions which make the order in which the dispositions were made and the evidentiary requirement of the testator's intention stand out as matters of some importance[49]. It would then have been appropriate in Scaevola's period for the question to be outlined more fully; the more so as the disposition of liberty is under a condition[50].

So much for Scaevola's first argument. (2) The second is more straightforward: what if Titius does not enter? Then Stichus becomes free and heir as a result of the substitution. This point is unproblematic: in a will all depends on the *caput et fundamentum,* institution of the heir. If he does not enter,

---

[45] F. *Pringsheim,* SZ 42 (1921) 655n5.

[46] The evidentiary requirements may be interpolated: *Buckland,* Slavery 468n2. The words *in obscuro* may be compilatorial (VIR III.662 1.47); they are found both in Marcian and Paul D40.4.10.1, and both texts belong to the Sabinian mass.

[47] *Voci,* DER II 581.

[48] Translations: (1) If a slave who has been legated is instructed to be free, he is free. But if he is first instructed to be free and then legated, if it is certainly the plain intention of the testator that he take away the gift of freedom, since it is accepted today that even a gift of freedom can be taken away, then I think he falls to the legacy. But if there is uncertainty, then it is more favourable to say that he will be free. (2) If the same slave has been legated and instructed to be free, freedom takes priority: yet if he has both been legated in a later document and clear revocation of freedom is shown, the legacy will prevail on account of the testator's intention.

[49] For the various views *Voci,* DER II 570-, 578-.

[50] It is as well to note too that the words *libertatem accepit* are a complete misrepresentation of the position: if it were true that the slave had received his liberty already then there would be no need even to think about the legacy. This is another indication of defective reasoning in the text.

the other dispositions fail. All, that is, except the substitution, which of course is intended to provide for the very eventuality that the heir does not enter[51].

(3) The last argument is that so long as Stichus does not enter the estate in accordance with the *iussum* of the legatee then he is not taken to be the property of the legatee, and it is therefore certain that he is not heir[52]. Consequently the substitution applies, and Stichus becomes free and heir. This argument too is unobjectionable. But it is curious that here for the first time in the text it is indicated that the legacy and institution *sine libertate* would have operated to make Stichus heir, and through him to vest the share of the estate in Maevius. This is stated not to happen, but the possibility of its happening if the *iussum* is given is presupposed. In this respect there is a certain unevenness in the text, which otherwise concentrates on the invalidity of the legacy owing to the priority given to liberty. In other words, in this text the only case in which the legacy is not regarded as automatically void is the case in which owing to the failure of the *iussum* (or the failure of the heir to enter) there is no question but that the substitution must operate anyway.

It is at this point that the approval of Julian for the argument is cited. The approval is generally excavated from Ulp. D28.6.10.7, which was discussed above. This is unsatisfactory. The difference between the two texts was pointed out above: in Scaevola's case there is a legacy, as a result of which it may be possible to regard the words *si Stichus heres non erit, Stichus liber heresque esto* as a valid substitution on account of a material difference between institution and substitution. Yet those very words are stated in Ulpian-Julian to constitute an invalid substitution. It is scarcely possible to suppose that Scaevola appended in support of his argument a reference to a discussion which contradicted it.

Two more attractive possibilities suggest themselves. The first, that the reference is to a different text of Julian, which does not survive. It is by no means unlikely that in the course of a longer discussion Julian may have mentioned points which would have a more positive bearing on Scaevola's concerns in this text. The second, that the reference to Julian was added by another hand, attached to a person who failed to appreciate the difference between the two

---

[51] The Basilica text differs from the Digest, and the difference is relevant here. It changes subject in the course of the substitution clause, mentioning the free heir (Titius, whom it calls Petrus) in the protasis and the slave (Stichus, whom it calls Paulus) in the apodosis. This is equivalent to *si Petrus heres non erit, Paulus liber heresque esto*. This change of person immediately disposes of the *causa* and *gradus* problem. The result is that the question in the Basilica is reduced to Scaevola's second argument.

[52] The text here is rather unclear: it may be as well to insert with *Mommsen* so that it reads as follows: *porro quamdiu non adit <Titius, etiam Stichus non adibit> iussu legatarii* ... This brings the third argument into closer conjunction with the second but makes no serious difference: without the insertion, the text attributes Stichus' failure to become heir directly to the lack of Maevius' *iussum*; with the insertion, this is taken back a stage further and attributed to Titius' failure to enter. In the first of these cases Stichus can become only coheir with Titius, while in the second he becomes sole heir. But which of these the text is considering is not made clear.

cases. This (perhaps more drastic) possibility may find some support in the peculiarity of the words *hoc autem quod sentimus Iulianus quoque in libris suis probat: sentimus* to describe a jurist's opinion is remarkable (perhaps a connexion with *sententia* was intended?); the expression *in libris suis probat* is unique[53]. There is no shortage of citations, mostly in Ulpian, in the form *Pomponius libro quinto ex Sabino probat* which may serve some useful purpose in locating the passage referred to, but the vague expression here is unparalleled[54].

IV

How much of the text is to be attributed to Scaevola? And to whom are the non-Scaevolan elements to be assigned? First a list of doubtful elements:

(1) it seems unlikely that Scaevola could have regarded the matter of *gradus* and *causa* as the main issue, or that he could have discussed it in such a laborious, fruitless, and inaccurate way;

(2) *et quidem in plerisque quaeritur... et respondetur:* the association with the language of *responsa* is curious; *in plerisque* is odd: does it mean 'in several cases' or 'in the work of several persons' (for which *apud plerosque* would be preferable)? And if 'cases', what cases other than the present one? In two other texts, Ulp. D17.2.26 and Paul D17.2.25, the meaning is evidently 'cases'; in Marcel. D35.2.57 it is unclear. There are no further examples.

(3) *secundum haec proposita quaestio manifestetur* followed by the repetition of the will. The repetition is odd; odder since it follows the announcement that the problem is about to be elucidated. What about *proposita*? It is not clear whether it is intended to be read with *haec* or with *quaestio*. Although *secundum ea quae proponerentur* is very common in Scaevola's *responsa,* and *secundum haec* is also found, there is no example in the Digest in the form *secundum haec proposita*. Further, *manifestetur* is unusual: the only other passive use of the word in Scaevola relates to the elucidation of the *voluntas testatoris,* a context to which the word seems better suited. In other jurists the term is frequently used for law which has 'emerged', become established by rescript and so on. The use in Scaevola is both unique and inappropriate[55].

(4) *nos didicimus ... cum unus gradus videtur.* The premise of this circular argument is not likely to be Scaevolan. *Nos didicimus* is found only here; *disco* is altogether rare[56].

---

[53] VIR s.v. *liber* II.2 col.1584 11.38-43.

[54] This (random) example is taken from Ulp. D7.1.12.2 lib 17 ad Sabinum. The apparent parallel cases found in Iav. D40.7.28.1 *in libris Gaii Cassii scriptum est* and Iav. D46.3.78 *in libris Gaii scriptum est* are in fact a different matter: both are taken from his *libri ex Cassio* so can be supposed in their original context to have been easily referred to the text of Cassius.

[55] Scaev. D33.7.27.2 is the other example: VIR s.h.v. but *W. Kalb,* Roms Juristen nach ihrer Sprache dargestellt (Leipzig, 1890) 105 discusses the usage without objections.

(5) the reference to Julian is suspect, unless it is to a text which we do not possess.

These objections are not intended to recall the 'Interpolationenjagd' of the first decades of this century. Nor should they, since the most telling objections, (1) and (4), depend not on any hypothetical standards of linguistic purity but on serious inconsistencies in the text or on the impossibility of attributing a particular doctrine to a jurist of Scaevola's period.

At whose door are these interpolations to be laid? On the basis of a constitution of Justinian, C6.27.5 (cited above), which deals with a similar problem, alteration of the text has sometimes been associated with Justinian[57]. There is no doubt that this constitution could have affected the compilers' treatment of the text, since it ruled that an institution of one's slave without a gift of liberty must now be taken to imply a gift of liberty[58]. Another constitution which decreed that legacies could validly precede the *heredis institutio* in a will could also have motivated compilatorial interference with the text[59].

Yet the constitution has not been systematically applied to the text. In the part which discusses the consequences of Titius' failing to enter the inheritance, it is stated that Stichus as a result becomes free and heir on the basis of the substitution. But if the doctrine that institution *sine libertate* implied freedom was being applied, then Stichus could become free and heir on the basis of the institution; indeed there would be no consequences if Titius failed to enter. When this point in the text has remained untouched by Justinian's legislation, it is less plausible to attribute to him far-reaching interference and the suppression of now-obsolete argument in an earlier part of the text.

There are elements in the text too which can hardly be attributed to the compilers. The laborious argument on the change of *causa* is not to be expected of them: for such additions their time was short, and to fill out the text with quasi-jurisprudential reflections was not their brief. The same may be said for the circular argument on the priority given to liberty.

Similar characteristics are found in both passages. The first attempts to classify the cases where *causa* changes. It is bare of content, and its abstractness leads into faulty generalisations. Yet formally (and therefore superficially) the discussion is by no means so unimpressive: it produces a case in which the self-substitution is invalid, and then proceeds to consider the possibilities where conditions are involved. Structural strength masks material deficiency. It is the

---

[56] An expression of the post-classical law schools? *Beseler, SZ* 66 (1948) 288-9.

[57] K. H. *Schindler*, Justinians Haltung zur Klassik (Köln-Graz, 1966) 311-7 esp. 316n114.

[58] C6.27.5.1b (AD 531): ... *quare non hoc et in hereditate et humanius et favore libertatis inducimus, ut si quis servum suum scripserit heredem sine libertate omnimodo civis Romanus efficiatur?* ...

[59] C6.23.24 (AD 528) cf. Inst. 2.20.34; *Voci* DER II 580n53.

same with the argument for giving Stichus liberty. Its logical tightness gives conviction to its conclusion, but all this is show since beneath lurks a banal *petitio principii*. The step-by-step development in both passages and the rather academic character especially of the first may suggest a school origin. So might *nos didicimus*. The poor quality of the content will not however suggest a very good school.

If this suggestion is combined with a previous hypothesis, the picture which emerges is of a law school, stronger on form than on content and aspiring to logical methods. Works of classical law are available, although in this case it is not clear whether it is Julian's *digesta* which are being employed or the citation of Julian in Ulpian's *libri ad Sabinum*.

Beyond this for the moment we shall not go. Some elements may be attributed to the schools. The origin of others and of the problem in the text is not clear. Solutions to these questions may emerge from the treatment of other texts in the *liber singularis*. So far it is necessary only that the reader believe that considerable tracts of this text are not from the *stilus* of Scaevola, and that they are scarcely to be attributed to the compilers either.

4. Pal.187.2: D28.6.48.2[60]

Si pupillus substitutum sibi servum alienaverit eumque emptor liberum heredemque instituerit, numquid iste in substitutione habeat substitutum *universum? ut si quidem pupillus ad pubertatem pervenerit, necessarius ex testamento emptoris heres **exstitit, sin vero intra pubertatem decesserit, ex substitutione quidem liber et heres sit et necessarius patri pupilli, emptori autem voluntarius heres **exstitit.

*universum] sibi servum *Mo.*   **exstitit] existat *Mo.*

A pupil has sold the slave who is his pupillary substitute. The buyer has instituted the same slave heir *cum libertate*. The question is whether the slave remains pupillary substitute. Scaevola distinguishes according to whether the pupil reaches puberty: if so then the slave can be the *heres necessarius* of the buyer; if not then he will be required as the *necessarius* to the pupil's father, but may still become voluntary heir to the buyer.

The problem is plain, a conflict between the slave's two intended roles as *heres necessarius*. The principle that the pupillary substitution should take precedence was accepted before Scaevola.

---

[60] Translation: If a pupil has sold a slave who was substituted to him, and the buyer has instituted the slave heir with freedom, is it really so that in the case of substitution the pupil has the slave as substitute? As [?], if the pupil has reached puberty, the slave can be the *heres necessarius* in the buyer's will; but if the pupil has died before reaching puberty, on the basis of the substitution the slave may be free and *heres necessarius* to the pupil's father, but only voluntary heir to the buyer.

Ulp. D40.7.2.4 lib 4 ad Sabinum[61]. Quocumque gradu pupillo servus cum libertate substitutus sit necessarii causam optinet: quae sententia utilitatis causa recepta est et a nobis probatur. Celsus quoque putat libro quinto decimo cum libertate substitutum statuliberi causam optinere.

Regardless how remote the substitution of the slave may be, he is to be treated as a *necessarius*. Ulpian does not offer his opinion on the view of Celsus that the slave is a *statuliber*. Yet if his status as *necessarius* (qua substitute) must be respected then it is true to say that he is alienated *cum sua causa*, which is the hallmark of the *statuliber*. The view that such a slave was a *statuliber* had been adopted according to Papinian by *prudentes* whom he does not name[62]. How this worked in a different case is shown by Ulpian[63], who discusses the case that a slave had been legated yet appointed pupillary substitute: when the condition on the substitution materialises, *evancescit legatum*[64].

The closest parallel to Scaevola's discussion however is found in a text of Neratius. Here too priority is given to the slave's role as pupillary substitute.

Ner. D28.5.55 lib 1 membranarum[65]. Pater filio impuberi servum heredem substituit liberumque esse iussit: eum pupillus vendidit Titio: Titius eum iam primo testamento

---

[61] Translation: In whatever degree a slave has been substituted with freedom to a pupil, he has the status of *heres necessarius*: this view is accepted on practical grounds and I approve it. Celsus also suggests in book 15 that a slave substituted with freedom is a *statuliber*.

[62] Pap. D40.7.36 lib 2 definitionum; Justinian also notes in C6.27.5.3b (AD531) that the *veteres* regarded a slave substituted *cum libertate* to a pupil as a *statuliber*. The motivation, as in the text of Ulpian cited, is expressly stated by Papinian to be *utilitas*. This is interpreted by both J. A. Ankum, Symbolae David (Leiden, 1968) I.25 and U. Leptien, SDHI 35 (1969) 61 to be equivalent in this case to saving the slave's freedom *favore libertatis*. But Papinian states that it is in order that the father's will (*secundae tabulae*) should not fail owing to actions taken by his son while a pupil.

[63] Ulp. D28.6.18.1 lib 16 ad Sabinum.

[64] More common in the texts is the problem of a slave legated but given freedom by the pupillary substitute. Since in this case the slave himself is not the substitute, there is no danger of the will failing on his account, so the question how to resolve the conflict between legacy and liberty is more difficult. Was such a slave a *statuliber*? The Sabinians split on this point, Cassius denying but Julian maintaining it (Ulp. D40.7.2.1 lib 4 ad Sabinum). As for the legacy: (1) Jul. D30.81.10 lib 32 digestorum states that once the pupil had reached puberty (so that the *secundae tabulae* with the gift of liberty became invalid) the legatee could vindicate the slave; yet if the pupil died before that the slave became free. (2) Ulp. D40.7.2.2 reports Julian as saying *praevalere libertatis dationem*. This is vague, but does it mean that the legacy is void? Surely not, if we are to interpret it in consistency with D30.81.10: it must mean that if the substitution takes effect together with the gift of freedom to the slave then that must take priority over the legacy. (3) Pomp. D28.6.16pr lib 3 ad Sabinum says that the slave will be free on the principle that the *novissima scriptura* prevails. Again it is unclear whether Pomponius means that the legacy becomes void when the substitution and gift of liberty materialise or is void *ab initio* owing to an ensuing gift of liberty. This second view might seem odd since it is by no means clear that the substitution will ever take effect, but it could perhaps be justified on the view that *primae* and *secundae tabulae* form one will only: Gai. D29.3.11 lib 11 ad legem Iuliam et Papiam; Iav. D42.5.28 lib 1 epistularum; Ulp. D28.6.2.4 lib 6 ad Sabinum.

[65] Translation: A father substituted to his pupil son a slave as heir and instructed him to be free: the pupil sold him to Titius. Titius had already made a will, but in a second one instructed the slave to be free and heir. The earlier will of Titius is void both because the slave can become

facto in secundo testamento liberum heredemque esse iussit. superius testamentum Titii ruptum est quia is servus et heres potest esse et, ut superius testamentum rumpatur, sufficit ita posterius factum esse ut aliquo casu potuerit ex eo heres existere. quod ad vim autem eius institutionis pertinet, ita se res habet, ut quamdiu pupillo ex ea substitutione heres potest esse, ex Titii testamento libertatem hereditatemque consequi non possit: si pupillus in suam tutelam pervenerit, perinde ex Titii testamento liber heresque sit ac si pupillo substitutus non fuisset: si pupillo heres exstitit, propius est ut Titio quoque si velit heres esse possit.

The case gives more detail particularly with regard to the voiding of the testator's first will, but is in essentials identical. Scaevola's version is in comparison with Neratius' both compact and abstract. There is similar language in both texts, but no terms so unusual as to demonstrate that Neratius is the source for the Scaevolan text.

As for the form and argument of the text of Scaevola: formally it is most inelegant: the subject changes abruptly from the pupil to the substitute. The construction with *ut* following the question is rather unusual. Otherwise the only oddities are the indicative *exstitit* and *iste*[66], apparently intended to denote the pupil. As for argument, there is none. No appeal is made to *utilitas*, as is done in the texts of Papinian and Ulpian. On the other hand this is a particularly Severan concern[67].

5. Pal.188pr-1: D32.103pr-1[68]

Si pater exheredato filio *substituit heredem extraneum deinde ille extraneus hunc filium heredem instituit et heres factus intra pubertatem decedat, puto a substituto ei filio omnino legata praestari non debere quia non directo sed per successionem ad filium hereditas patris pervenit. (1) Plus ego in fratre, qui cum heres exstitisset patri exheredatum fratrem heredem instituit, accepi substitutum eius legatum non debere ac ne quidem si intestato fratri successerit quia non principaliter sed per successionem bona **fratris ad eum pervenerunt.

*substituit] instituit *Cujas*   **fratris] patris *Cujas*

---

heir, and because in order to render it void it is sufficient for a subsequent will to be made in such a way that in some case an heir can be appointed on the basis of it. But as for the force of the institution, the situation is that so long as the slave can be substitute heir to the pupil, he cannot obtain his freedom and the inheritance from Titius' will; but if the pupil reaches majority, the slave can be free and heir through Titius' will just as if he had never been substituted to the pupil. If he does become heir to the pupil, it is better to say that he may also become heir to Titius if he wishes.

[66] *Beseler*, Beiträge III 133.

[67] The conclusion of both *Ankum*, Symbolae David 7; and *Leptien*, SDHI 35 (1969) 71-2.

[68] Translation (with *Cujas'* emendations): If a father has disinherited his son and instituted an heir outside the family, and then that heir has instituted the son as his heir, and the son has become heir and died before reaching puberty: I think that legacies are not payable at all by a substitute to the son, since the father's estate came to the son not directly but by way of succession. (1) Furthermore I accepted that, in the case of a brother who had become heir to his father and had instituted his disinherited brother as his heir, the substitute of the second brother does not owe legacies, not even if the second brother has succeeded the first on intestacy, since his father's property came to him not directly but by way of succession.

I

D32.103 is discussed in the following two sections: in this one, the *principium* and § 1 which are concerned with legacies in the *secundae tabulae* when the pupil has been disinherited; in the next, §§ 2 and 3 which cover the case that the pupil has been instituted.

The first difficulty in the *principium* emerges as we try to elucidate the facts. F (a father) has disinherited P (his pupil son); instituted H (a non-family heir) and also substituted H to P. F dies and H enters his estate. H then institutes P his heir; H dies and P enters his estate, which now of course includes F's estate. P dies, still under age. It is time for the pupillary substitute, but H is dead. His death however is inconvenient since the rest of the problem depends on his continued well-being.

What the problem demands is that the testator's heir (H), whose death is recorded in the course of the problem, should not be the same person as the pupillary substitute (S). The simplest means of reaching this result is to adopt Cujas' ingenious reading[69], *instituit* for *substituit*. So sense is restored: F disinherits P, institutes H, substitutes S to P[70]. Then F dies, H enters and later institutes P. H dies, and P enters. P dies as a pupil, and S, the pupillary substitute, acquires the estate. Scaevola's question arises now, as legatees under F's will attempt to claim their legacies[71].

Should the legacies be paid by the substitute? Scaevola answers no, his reason that the substitute acquired the estate not directly but by way of succession to another party. The context of this argument can be supplied from other texts[72]:

Jul. D35.2.87.7 lib 61 digestorum. Qui filios impuberes duos habebat alterum heredem instituit alterum exheredavit, deinde exheredatum instituto substituit ac postea ex-

---

[69] Observationes 2.32.

[70] This point is of course not present in the text as emended. But it must be construed, given (1) the need for there to be a substitute in this problem who (2) is a different person from the heir.

[71] These must be legatees under the *secundae tabulae*: if they were in the *primae* they would be charged on the heir (H) and so not relevant later on in the problem.

[72] Translations: (Julian) A man who had two pupil sons instituted one heir and disinherited the other, and then substituted the disinherited son to the instituted one, and in turn Maevius to the disinherited son and charged legacies on him (Maevius): the disinherited son became heir to his pupil brother and died while still himself a pupil. Since owing to the father's intention his property came to him (Maevius) through succession by way of substitution, it can be said that the legacies charged on him must be paid after taking the *lex Falcidia* into account for the property which the father had at the time of his death. And it is not contrary to this that, although the father has given a legacy to the disinherited son, the obligation of the substitute towards the legacies is not in any way increased, since in this case it was not a share of the estate but a legacy which came to him. Someone will say: what if the disinherited son did not become heir to his brother through the substitution, but on intestacy or through an intermediary, and then died as a pupil? Must the substitute then also be regarded as owing the legacies? No: for the great difference between the case where the disinherited son becomes heir to his brother

heredato Maevium et ab eo legavit: et exheredatus fratri impuberi exstitit heres deinde impubes decessit. cum iudicio patris facultates paternae per causam hereditariam ex substitutione ad eum perveniant, potest dici legata ab eo relicta praestanda esse habita ratione legis Falcidiae in his bonis quae pater mortis tempore reliquerit. nec huic contrarium est quod, cum exheredato pater legatum dederit, nihilo magis substitutus legatis obligabitur, quia eo casu non hereditatis paternae portio sed legatum ad eum pervenit. dicet aliquis: quid ergo si exheredatus filius non ex substitutione fratri suo heres exstiterit sed aut lege aut per interpositam personam atque ita impubes decesserit? sic quoque existimandus erit substitutus legata debere? minime: nam quantum intersit exheredatus filius ex substitutione fratri suo heres exsistat an alio modo vel ex eo apparet quod alias ab eo legare pater potuit, alias non potuit. est igitur rationi congruens ne plus iuris circa personam substituti testator habeat quam habuerat in eo cui eum substituebat.

Pap. D35.2.11.8 lib 29 quaestionum. Si quis exheredato filio substituit heredem institutum et ab eo tabulis quoque secundis legaverit, necessario ratio confundetur cum ideo legata valere dixerit Iulianus a substituto relicta, quod idem patri heres exstiterit.

Julian's text envisages a situation similar to that in Scaevola: one pupil son is instituted, the other disinherited but substituted to his brother; the disinherited pupil in turn is given a substitute from whom legacies are left. The disinherited pupil became substitute and died while still *impubes*: are the legacies due? Julian's response is that they are since they come to the substitute *per causam hereditariam ex substitutione.* Later the question whether the legacies would be due if the disinherited son had become heir not by substitution but on intestacy or through an intermediary receives a negative answer: such legacies would not be due from the disinherited son himself let alone from his substitute[73].

---

through the substitution and other cases is plain from the fact that in the one case the father can charge legacies and in the other cannot. It is therefore rational that the testator should not have more rights in the person of the substitute than he had in the son to whom he substituted him.

(Papinian) If someone disinherited his son and substituted to him the person whom he had himself instituted heir and left legacies from him in the pupillary will too, the reckoning necessarily becomes merged into one, as Julian says that legacies left from the substitute are valid on the ground that the same person has become heir to the father.

[73] Not directly relevant to the point at issue in Scaevola is the question whether legacies charged on a substitute would be due if a legacy had been left to the pupil by his father. But the matter deserves brief consideration since it is raised in this text of Julian. The general principle is that legacies could not validly be charged on the substitute of a disinherited pupil: Paul D30.126pr lib sing de secundis tabulis. *Fideicommissa* on the other hand, until a constitution of Justinian (C6.37.24 of AD531), could probably be charged on the substitute of a disinherited pupil, provided the pupil had received something under the will (see *P. de Francisci,* BIDR 22 (1910) 197-203; *K. H. Schindler,* Justinians Haltung zur Klassik (Köln-Graz, 1966) 236-240). This rule seems clear and firm. It is not however in my view the point at issue in this text of Julian. The relevant words are *nec huic ... pervenit.* Since a legacy charged on a legatee was plainly invalid (G2.271) it would be of no particular interest to state that the substitute of a pupil who had been disinherited but given a legacy under the will could not be burdened with legacies. The point is rather this: the text remains concerned with the same problem (the pupil has been disinherited but substituted, a substitute has in turn been appointed to him, and so on) with one addition, that a legacy has now been left to the pupil. Consequently the pupillary substitute can, through the pupil, acquire the paternal estate plus the legacy. Julian's point is that this further acquisition, since it comes to him as a legacy not as a share of the estate, does

Papinian produces a different case, since in it the father's heir is also the pupillary substitute. Legacies left here from the pupillary substitute are valid. The reason is attributed to Julian, that legacies charged on a substitute are valid when he has become heir to the testator.

Yet these cases are best seen as exceptions against the stark background sketched by Paul: *ab exheredati substituto inutiliter legatum datur.* (D30.126pr, discussed more fully below). In Papinian's case the exception is made because the substitute is the testator's heir, and just as it is admissible to burden him with legacies in the *primae tabulae,* so too it is allowed to charge them on him in the *secundae tabulae*: the effect is simply to make the payment of those legacies conditional on the death of the pupil during puberty[74]. In Julian's case the substitute came into possession of the testator's estate as a direct consequence of a series of institutions and substitutions provided for by the testator. What the two cases have in common is that the property reached the substitute as a result of the testator's intention[75]. It is this intentionality which rescues the legacies from the invalidity otherwise pronounced on them by Paul.

Scaevola's decision appears to rest on the same basis: it is plain that the substitute did not come into possession of the property purely as a consequence of provisions made by the testator (F). Rather his acquisition depends as much on the chance circumstance of the pupil's having been instituted heir by H. It is not possible for the testator (F) to foresee that his estate will end in the hands of S, and it is this loose connexion which gives the legatees such a poor claim, which ultimately fails. So far as can be seen the testator envisaged that the substitute should obtain only the pupil's property[76] and never imagined him as his own heir.

What would have prompted the legatees' claim in the first place? The conception that legacies in the *secundae tabulae* are to be treated like those in the *primae tabulae.* As Papinian says, *quae tabulis secundis relinquuntur quasi primis sub condicione relicta intelleguntur,* and the idea that both lots of *tabulae* together form one will is found in several texts[77]. If this view is taken then the *dies cedens* of the legacies has passed, and this is expressly stated by Ulpian[78]. It is presumably this that inspired the legatees to attempt their claim. Yet the fact that they have a legitimate claim does not of itself enable them to bring it against anyone who

---

not in any way increase his liability to pay out legacies: that is what *nihilo magis substitutus legatis obligabitur* means (cf. Iav. D35.2.60 lib 14 ex Cassio).

[74] Pap. D35.2.11.5 lib 29 quaestionum ad fin.

[75] For the importance of intention cf. Paul D32.6.1 lib 1 fideicommissorum.

[76] And he surely cannot have supposed that this would amount to very much: cf. G2.182.

[77] Pap. D35.2.11.5; Gai. D29.3.11; Iav. D42.5.28; Ulp. D28.6.2.4; *K. A. von Vangerow,* Lehrbuch der Pandekten⁷ II (Marburg-Leipzig, 1867) §521n2.

[78] Ulp. D36.2.7.4 and 5 lib 20 ad Sabinum.

II

The position in § 1 is very similar[80]. One son has been instituted, the other disinherited. Two variants follow. In the first the disinherited son is instituted heir by his brother and on the successive deaths of his father and his brother acquires his brother's estate, which now includes his father's. On his death *impubes* the substitute acquires the estate. In the second variant there is no will, so that the acquisition of the estate by the disinherited son is as *proximus adgnatus* of his brother. It is the same question for both variants: does the substitute owe legacies? Scaevola denies this since the father's property came to him not *principaliter* but through succession[81].

The first variant may be left aside since it does not differ from the case in the *principium*. As for intestacy, Paul provides a clear statement[82]:

> Paul D30.126pr lib sing de secundis tabulis. Ab exheredati substituto inutiliter legatum datur. ergo nec a legitimo exheredati fideicommissum dari poterit, quod et legitimi eo iure praestare coguntur quo si scripti fuissent. sed si committente aliquo ex liberis edictum praetoris quo contra tabulas bonorum possessionem pollicetur, scriptus quoque filius contra tabulas bonorum possessionem petierit, substitutus eius legata pro modo patrimonii quod ad filium pervenit praestabit, perinde ac si id quod per bonorum possessionem filius habuit a patre accepisset.

The latter part of this text is more relevant to the next section, in which *bonorum possessio* is discussed. But the general point made at the beginning is important here. It is taken for granted that a legacy charged on the pupil's intestate heir would be void, but so in this case would a *fideicommissum*. If we work on the principle that *fideicommissa* can be charged on any beneficiary

---

[79] A related question is the payability of debts of the paternal estate by the pupillary substitute. Ulp. D29.2.42pr lib 4 disputationum (citing Julian and Marcellus) shows that this was controversial: he deals with abstention by, rather than disherison of, a pupil, and Julian's view that the substitute must stand liable for all the father's debts is criticised as impractical. But Julian's view is also that of Iavolenus: see Iav. D42.5.28 with the remarks of *B. Eckardt*, Iavoleni epistulae (Berlin, 1978) 136-144.

[80] 'Wertlose Dublette': *Beseler*, SZ 44 (1924) 360.

[81] It is necessary here, with *Cujas* Observationes 2.32, to read *patris* in place of *fratris:* for it is true to say that the father's property has been acquired by the disinherited son *non principaliter sed per successionem*, but the same is not true of the brother's property.

[82] Translation: A legacy cannot validly be charged on the substitute of a disinherited son. Therefore a *fideicommissum* cannot be charged on the intestate heir of a disinherited son, because intestate heirs too are compelled to pay bequests on the same principle as if they had been instituted. But if one child invokes *bonorum possessio contra tabulas* in the praetor's edict, a son instituted heir may also seek it, and his substitute will then pay legacies in accordance with the share of the estate which came to the son, just as if the son had received from his father the share which came to him by *bonorum possessio*.

under a will or on intestacy[83], but conversely cannot be charged on someone who receives no benefit, then it is clear that the sort of *fideicommissum* considered by Paul cannot be valid since the intestate heir of the disinherited pupil cannot be said to have received any benefit from the testator[84].

So much for *fideicommissa*. In the text of Scaevola however it appears to be legacies which are in question, and there is no need for further argument here to demonstrate that legacies could not be charged on a disinherited pupil's intestate heir.

6. Pal.188.2-3: D32.103.2-3[85]

Si filius ex uncia heres institutus sit et ab eo legata data sint, habeat et substitutum, deinde commisso edicto per alium filium accepit partis dimidiae bonorum possessionem: substitutus eius utrum ex uncia legata praestat an vero ex semisse? et verius est ex semisse *sed ex uncia omnibus ex reliquis liberis et parentibus. (3) Contra quoque si ex dodrante institutus commisso edicto **semissem acceperit bonorum possessionem, ex semisse tantum legata substitutus debebit: quo modo enim augentur ubi amplius est in bonorum possessione, sic et ubi minus est deducitur.

*sed ex uncia omnibus ex reliquis *del. Mo.*   **semissem] ex semisse *Hal.*

A pupil is instituted to one twelfth of his father's estate and legacies are charged on him. His brother claims *bonorum possessio contra tabulas*, and consequently each ends up with half the estate. The question arises after the pupil has died in puberty and been succeeded by his substitute whether legacies are to be paid *ex uncia* or *ex semisse*. The problem in § 3 is precisely the same except that the pupil, owing to *bonorum possessio contra tabulas*, has had his share reduced from three quarters to a half.

The principles are these. After *b. p. contra tabulas* the will (*primae tabulae*) although still valid at civil law was in effect set aside by the praetor's decree. Hence the legacies were not paid. Yet it was thought to be more equitable that certain family members should nonetheless receive their legacies[86]. A claimant or recipient of *b. p. contra tabulas* had therefore to pay legacies *liberis parentibusque*.

---

[83] Ulp. D32.1.6 lib 1 fideicommissorum; Paul D32.6.1 lib 1 fideicommissorum.

[84] The same principle is followed by Jul. D30.94pr lib 39 digestorum, who states that a *fideicommissum* charged on the intestate heir of a disinherited pupil is not payable unless the intestate heir should also be the heir of the pupil's father.

[85] Translation: If a son has been instituted heir to a twelfth, and legacies have been charged on him, and he also has a substitute; and then another son invokes the edict, as a result of which he receives *bonorum possessio* of half the estate: should his substitute pay legacies in accordance with a twelfth share or a half? It is better to say in accordance with a half share, [but with a twelfth to all others, children and relatives.] (3) But if he has been instituted to a three-quarter share and after the edict has been invoked has received *bonorum possessio* of a half, the substitute will owe legacies only in accordance with a half share. For just as legacies are increased where the share in *bonorum possessio* is greater, so also where there is less there is a reduction.

[86] Ulp. D37.5.1pr lib 40 ad edictum.

For the substitute of a pupil who had obtained *b. p. contra tabulas* the position was different: the *secundae tabulae* were given effect and therefore all legacies were due[87].

Several texts discuss the effect on legacies if the share to which a *filius* has been instituted has been amended upwards or downwards as a consequence of *b. p. contra tabulas*. They are unanimous in stating that legacies are payable in accordance with the actual share received rather than that specified in the will. This applies both to the case that the legacies are charged on a pupil[88] and that they are charged on his substitute[89].

There are two views to consider on the legacies in this text. (1) *Cujas* thought that the legacies discussed were charged on the substitute[90]. He proposed the elegant solution (for his view) of transposing *et ab eo legata data sint* to follow *habeat et substitutum*. If this view is followed then Scaevola's solution would be expected to be that the substitute owed legacies to all *ex semisse*. Hence the words *sed ex uncia omnibus ex reliquis liberis et parentibus* must be expunged. They are in any case vague and confusing[91]. (2) If the view of *Cujas* is rejected then the legacies are to be understood to be charged on the pupil[92]. The substitute has therefore inherited liability to pay them, and pays not *suo nomine* but *defuncti pupilli nomine*[93]. He can be liable to pay only those which the pupil was liable to pay, that is those *liberis parentibusque*. On this view Scaevola's solution would be expected to be that the substitute owed legacies *ex semisse* only *liberis parentibusque*. In this case it is only the words *sed ex uncia omnibus ex reliquis* which need be expunged.

Which version is more plausible? For the second speak the fact that no emendation of the text is required, and that the words *sed ... reliquis* are intelligible alone as a single comment or gloss. The same cannot be said for the words *sed ... parentibus*. On the other hand almost all other discussions relate to payment of legacies charged on the substitute (see note 89); that is in itself more problematic than the straightforward question of inheriting liability to an obligation of the pupil; and the preceding sections of D32.103 deal with the payment of legacies charged on a substitute. On the whole I should favour *Cujas'* view. The matter however is hardly to be decided, a state of affairs which reflects the fact that it is not the main problem of the text. That is rather the proportion in accordance with which the legacies are payable, and since that question is

---

[87] Afr. D28.6.34.2 lib 4 quaestionum.

[88] Afr. D28.6.35 lib 5 quaestionum.

[89] Ulp. D37.5.5pr-1 lib 40 ad edictum; Afr. D28.6.35; Paul D30.126pr lib sing de secundis tabulis (quoted above).

[90] Observationes 3.9.

[91] 'sunt ignari et inepti cuiusdam interpretis' (*Cujas* loc.cit.).

[92] *Faber*, Coniecturae 5.1.

[93] Cf. Jul. D35.2.87.4 lib 61 digestorum (in which however there is no *b.p. contra tabulas*).

decided in the same way for both pupil and substitute further discussion is not required. Equally, so far as the attempt to establish the nature of textual alterations in the LSQPT is concerned, the point is relatively unimportant since the identification of a gloss is unavoidable.

It is worth considering the point of the question whether legacies are due *ex uncia* or *ex semisse*. The text does not elaborate. If the pupil's share is increased sixfold, from a twelfth to a half, is it to be supposed that legacies will be increased proportionally? This is *a priori* most implausible. In the case of the pupil, the *primae tabulae* are although not void set aside: so payment at all by the pupil is already a special concession. As for the substitute, the natural equity which saves legacies for children and close relatives surely cannot extend to multiplication of legacies payable to outsiders. In my view the question of proportions is to be understood rather in relation to the *lex Falcidia*. There are several texts which support this proposition, mention of most of which is best left to a footnote[94]. One text which is closely parallel to that of Scaevola my be discussed more fully. It is regrettably corrupt, and is not transmitted in the Basilica.

Afr. D28.6.35 lib 5 quaestionum[95]. Etsi contra tabulas patris petita sit a pupillo bonorum possessio, in substitutum tamen eius actionem legati dandam esse ita ut augeantur praeter ea* quod filius extraneis non debuerit. sic et crescere a substituto data legata si per bonorum possessionem plus ad filium pervenisset, quemadmodum et ipse filius plus exceptis deberet. his consequens esse existimo ut, si impubes ex asse scriptus sit et per bonorum possessionem semis ei ablatus sit, substitutus in partem legati nomine exoneretur ut, quemadmodum portio quae per bonorum possessionem accesserit auget legata, ita et hic quae abscesserit minuat.

*praeter ea [legata quae peti non possunt propterea] quod *ins. Mo.*

---

[94] Two texts are plain: (1) Ulp. D37.5.5pr-1: here the words at the end of § 1 *licet enim ex uncia fuerit impubes institutus, tamen quod accessit augebit legata a substituto relicta* are found specifically in the context of the *ratio legis Falcidiae*; (2) Ulp. D37.5.5.5: the same may be said. Other texts are more difficult: (3) Ulp. D37.5.5.8 *id quod extraneis non praestatur liberis parentibusve profuturum non dubitamus:* since fewer legacies are payable, the Falcidian threshold of three quarters will not be reached so readily, so reduction of the legacies left to children and relatives will not be necessary. Similarly the words *igitur ita demum quod extraneis non praestatur communicatur cum eo qui contra tabulas petit si non legatariis liberis parentibusque dandum sit* indicate that an obligation to pay the legacies to children and relatives will be enforced by the praetor. Consequently the whole saving in not paying legacies to outsiders is not passed on to a co-recipient of *b.p. contra tabulas,* but only a share of what is left after the family members have been paid their legacies without any Falcidian reduction. (4) Paul D30.126pr: *legata pro modo patrimonii quod ad filium pervenit praestabit* i.e. the calculation for the *lex Falcidia* is made *pro modo patrimonii.*

[95] Translation: Although a pupil has sought *bonorum possessio contra tabulas* against his father's will, nonetheless an action for legacies must be given against the substitute, so that they are increased except for the ones which the son did not owe (to persons outside the family). In this way legacies charged on the substitute are also increased if more has come to the son through *bonorum possessio,* just as the son himself owed more to *exceptae personae.* I think it consistent with this that, if the pupil has been instituted sole heir and through *bonorum possessio* has had half taken away from him, the substitute should be relieved in part of the burden of legacies, so that just as where the share which accrues through *bonorum possessio* increases legacies, so here what is deducted should reduce them.

An action for legacies is to be given against the substitute, yet only for legacies to the family (the pupil would not have owed any others), which may be increased since those to outsiders are not payable. Two point are clear: (1) that the legacies are charged on the pupil, and the substitute has inherited liability to pay them; (2) that the sense in which the legacies may be increased (*augeantur*) is that the total of legacies is now reduced since outsiders are not paid, and therefore the amount payable in family legacies can be higher without infringing the *lex Falcidia*[96]. The text goes on to discuss a further case: legacies charged on the substitute increase if the son has through *b. p. contra tabulas* obtained a greater share of the estate. Here the text is plainly speaking of all legacies. We cannot therefore suppose that any form of increase is intended other than a more favourable reckoning under the *lex Falcidia*.

The parallel between these texts of Scaevola and Africanus is striking: they alone raise the question of reducing legacies if, after *b. p. contra tabulas*, it is a lower share that has been received; they end with similar generalisations: more is to be paid if more is received, less if less. The variations they describe are caused by the scale for calculating the Falcidian quarter[97]. Most texts do not mention these points; nor, strictly, need they: for the *lex Falcidia* applies automatically, and all that need be determined in advance for its application is whether it is the instituted share or the share received which is to be the base for the calculation.

There is a marked contrast between the generalisations of Scaevola and Africanus. Africanus is entirely clear; Scaevola is muddled and inelegant, since with *augentur* evidently *legata* is to be supplied, but just as clearly cannot be in the parallel clause with *deducitur*. Similarly *ubi amplius est in bonorum possessione* is a most unusual expression[98]. It is worth considering whether this last sentence of Scaevola may be derived from a reading of Africanus.

7. Pal.189: D35.2.96[99]

Miles si dum paganus erat fecerit testamentum, militiae tempore codicillos, lex Falcidia in codicillis locum non habet, in testamento locum habebit.

If a soldier has while a civilian made a will and during military service added codicils, then the *lex Falcidia* applies to legacies given in the will but not to those in the codicils.

---

[96] For the use of *augere* to describe the payment of increased legacies owing to a more favourable reckoning under the *lex Falcidia* cf. Jul. D35.2.87.5 and 8 lib 61 digestorum.

[97] In §2 the change from 1/12 to 1/2 corresponds to a modification of the total of due legacies from a maximum of 3/48 of the total estate to 18/48. In §3 the reduction from 3/4 to 1/2 demands a reduction from 9/16 to a maximum of 6/16 of the total estate.

[98] In the list of texts in which *in bonorum possessione esse* is found (VIR I.593 11.11-22) there is no parallel to this case: most of the examples there can be translated 'in the case of *b.p.*' They do not refer to property being 'in' *bonorum possessio*.

[99] Translation: If a soldier has made a will while a civilian but added codicils during military service, the *lex Falcidia* does not apply to the codicils but does to the will.

7. Pal.189: D35.2.96

The fragment is laconic: (a) legacies are not even mentioned; (b) no reference is made to the time of death; (c) it is not stated whether the codicils were confirmed or not. It is a classic example of extreme concision in presenting a legal problem. The lacunae mentioned can be filled: (a) the reference to the *lex Falcidia* makes plain that legacies are involved; (b) the statement that the will and codicils are to be treated differently indicates that the military disposition is still valid *iure militari* so that the testator must have died during service or within a year of honourable discharge; (c) since the question is raised whether the *lex Falcidia*, which applies to legacies, should apply to dispositions in the codicils, and since in unconfirmed codicils only *fideicommissa* are valid, it appears that the codicils must have been confirmed[100].

The problem in the text however is none of these. It is whether the *lex Falcidia* should apply both to the legacies in the will and those in the codicils; whether, that is, will and codicils should be treated under the same law (*ius*), civil or military. Scaevola decides against a uniform treatment. The will was made while a civilian and is to be interpreted *iure civili*. It follows that the *lex Falcidia* applies. The codicils were made during military service and are to be interpreted *iure militari*. It follows that the *lex Falcidia* does not apply to them[101].

This decision looks rational. But it is undogmatic.

Jul. D29.7.2.2 lib 37 digestorum[102]. Codicillorum ius singulare est ut quaecumque in his scribentur perinde haberentur ac si in testamento scripta essent ...

Or to take the same point from Scaevola[103]:

Scaev. D29.7.14pr lib 8 quaestionum ... codicilli pro parte testamenti habentur ...

On this principle the codicils ought to be read into the will, so that it is the time of making the will which is crucial and which then determines whether it is *ius civile* or *ius militare* which is to apply. If this approach were employed in the text of Scaevola then the argument would be that although the codicils were made during military service they have to be read into a will made under civil law and must consequently be interpreted under civil law. Hence the *lex Falcidia* would apply to all dispositions. But Scaevola does not appear to be tempted by this view. Nor does Gaius, who discusses the opposite case, where the will has been made during military service and the codicils afterwards while a civilian[104]:

---

[100] These points however depend on a strict reading of the language of this text: (1) on the tacit argument that reference to the *lex Falcidia* implies the involvement of legacies. But Justinian abolished the *SC Pegasianum*, and it cannot be certain that some texts did not refer originally to it rather than to the *lex Falcidia*. (2) In Scaevola confusion between legacies and *fideicommissa* is common (*Voci*, DER II 234n45).

[101] Ulp. D36.1.3.1 lib 3 fideicommissorum.

[102] Translation: (Julian) The particular law applying to codicils is that whatever is written in them is treated as if it had been written in the will.

[103] Translation: 'Codicils are treated as part of the will'. In this text Scaevola is reporting the views of Sabinus and Cassius, but the words cited appear to be regarded as an uncontroversial premise of the argument which follows. Cf. Gai. D29.3.11 lib 11 ad legem Iuliam et Papiam.

Gai. D29.1.17.4 lib 15 ad edictum provinciale. Si miles testamentum in militia fecerit, codicillos post militiam et intra annum missionis moriatur, plerisque placet in codicillis iuris civilis regulam spectari debere, quia non sunt a milite facti nec ad rem pertinere quod testamento confirmati sunt. ideoque in his legatis quae testamento data sunt legi Falcidiae locum non esse, at in his quae codicillis scripta sunt locum esse.

That the issue was disputed is indicated by the words *plerisque placet*; that the strict interpretation treating the codicils as part of the will was abandoned is shown by the words *nec ad rem pertinere quod testamento confirmati sunt*.

There is plenty of evidence for this treatment of dispositions in a will separately from those in codicils, if one was drawn up during military service and the other before or after. The texts record both positions: civil will and military codicils[105]; military will and civil codicils[106]. While the existence of the problem is not concealed, no dissenting voices are heard. The matter had apparently been resolved by the early classical period in favour of separate treatment of will and codicils.

When one reflects that the military will is composed not so much of a bundle of rules as of their absence, and that emperors at any rate had a vested interest in favouring the military, then it does not perhaps seem so very surprising that a strict interpretation was sacrificed here for a less rigorous one which preserved for the soldier a significant legal privilege[107].

On the form and argument of the fragment little comment is required. The extreme concision has already been remarked upon, a feature more characteristic of *responsa* than of a *quaestio*.

---

[104] Translation: If a soldier has made a will during military service and codicils after it, and then dies within a year of discharge from service, some think that the rule of civil law should apply to the codicils since they were not made by a soldier, and that it does not matter that they were confirmed in the will. And so the *lex Falcidia* does not apply to legacies left in the will, but it does apply to the codicils.

[105] Scaev. D35.2.96; Paul D29.7.8.4 lib sing de iure codicillorum where the point is specifically made that codicils made during service *non debent referri ad testamentum* (made under civil law). The qualification that the will is valid at civil law only if it was not sealed or supplemented during service is also worth noting. A. Guarino, 'Pauli de iure codicillorum liber singularis' SZ 62 (1942) 209-254 gives a short exegesis of this text at 244-5. It is unconvincing: *Guarino* emphasises the informality of the military will and does not believe in the existence of military codicils. But the problem is a conflict between civil and military law, and the question which *ius* to apply. In relation to this problem, the mention of military codicils seems acceptable. (*Guarino* cites *V. Arangio Ruiz*, BIDR 18 (1906) 160n3 (162) on D29.7.9.1; 29.7.20.1; 29.7.25. But these cases refer to the question whether a will which is void at civil law can convalesce through taking up military service.)

[106] Gai. D29.1.17.4 lib 15 ad edictum provinciale; Tryph. D29.1.18 lib 18 disputationum; Jul. D29.1.20pr lib 27 digestorum; Scaev. D35.2.17 lib 6 quaestionum.

[107] It is in some respects a curious privilege (a point I owe to Prof. Crook), since the non-applicability of the *lex Falcidia* might well increase the chances of an heir being unwilling to enter and so causing the will to fail. But the privilege is no doubt to be seen in the uninfringed validity of the *voluntas testatoris*.

8. Pal.190: D36.1.81[108]

Si pupillus parenti suo heres extitit et fideicommissam hereditatis partem restituit, mox abstinetur paterna hereditate: optio deferenda est fideicommissario ut aut portionem quoque pupilli adgnoscat aut toto discedat. aut omnimodo bona vendenda sunt ut id quod superfluum est pupillo servetur, et si in solidum bona venire non possunt omnimodo actiones fideicommissario denegandae erunt: erat enim in potestate illius universum suscipere et si quid plus erit pupillo servare.

I

A pupil becomes heir to his father and restores a *fideicommissum* of part of the estate. He then abstains from it. The fideicommissary is to have the choice between accepting the pupil's share as well as his own or rejecting both. The text falls into two parts, the first of which ends at *discedat*. The second part is left aside for the moment.

The praetor allowed a pupil to abstain from an estate even after meddling with it; all others lost the privilege of abstention by interference[109]. Here the pupil's action has apparently been limited to restoring the *fideicommissum*, but Ulpian makes clear that that was sufficient in itself to amount to meddling[110]. The power to abstain is preserved precisely because the meddling was done by a pupil[111].

As for the fideicommissary, the option put to him is most interesting. To have to choose between accepting all or nothing is precisely the choice that a coheir must make, if his coheir has declined to enter[112]: if he accepts his share, then the unoccupied one accrues to it. Otherwise he leaves empty-handed. That the treatment of the fideicommissary is analogous is significant. In his case and in that of coheirs, a decision to take nothing leads ultimately to cession of the estate for *bonorum venditio* by the creditors[113].

---

[108] Translation: If a pupil has become heir to his father and has made over a *fideicommissum* of part of the estate, and has then abstained from it: the fideicommissary must be given the choice whether to accept the pupil's share as well or to decline both. Or in any case the property is to be sold up so that the excess can be kept for the pupil, and if the property cannot be sold in full in any case the fideicommissary is to be refused actions, for it was in his power to take the whole and keep any excess for the pupil.

[109] Gai. D29.2.57pr lib 23 ad edictum provinciale: *Lenel*, EP 418–421 gives the two 'subedicts' of the edict *si suus heres erit*, for pupil and then for *pubes*.

[110] Ulp. D36.1.6.2 lib 4 fideicommissorum; cf. Jul. D36.1.28.3 lib 40 digestorum (corrupt).

[111] It is interesting to note that the privilege of abstention was retained in spite of the fact that the pupil's tutor must have authorised the restitution of the *fideicommissum*.

[112] Cf. S. *Solazzi*, BIDR 16 (1904) 99n4: Marci. D29.2.55 lib 2 regularum (where the parallel with Scaevola's language is particularly marked: *cum hereditate patris necessarius heres se abstineat, condicio coheredi sive suo sive extraneo defertur, ut aut totam adgnoscat aut a toto recedat*...; cf. also Ulp. (?) D29.2.56 lib 57 ad edictum, *condicio deferenda*); Pomp. D29.2.99 lib 1 senatus consultorum; Jul. D37.10.7.5 lib 24 digestorum (on the *edictum Carbonianum*); cf. Gai. D29.1.17.1 lib 15 ad edictum provinciale; Ulp. D29.2.38 lib 43 ad edictum; and in general Gai. D29.2.53.1 lib 14 ad legem Iuliam et Papiam.

Only the classical elements have been sketched until now: the *beneficium abstinendi*; the parallel between the cases of partial heir and fideicommissary to part of the estate. These are readily comprehensible, but the interpretation of this text presents difficulties. It is simplest to follow the classical lines a little further before approaching the text in detail. The two options would be construed as follows: (a) if the fideicommissary accepted the whole estate, then by assignment of actions in accordance with the *SC Trebellianum* he would be able to sue for debts owed to the estate and would be obliged to pay debts due from it. Acceptance of the whole in the face of abstention by the pupil cannot have been without risks (hence the power to choose). Yet if his reckoning was good then even after payment of all creditors he would register a gain on his acceptance of the whole; (b) if the fideicommissary refused, the estate would be put up for sale. After certain formalities the estate would as a whole be knocked down to the person who offered the highest percentage of repayment on the debts. This person, the *bonorum emptor,* also operated with risks (although lesser ones, since while legitimated to sue for full payment of debts due to the estate, he would hardly have offered 100% repayment of debts owed by it). A good calculation, that is paying the creditors as little as possible, might bring a handsome profit.

Whichever version applies, the end result is that the whole estate is in the hands of one person (fideicommissary or *bonorum emptor*) and the creditors are paid by him. The pupil after his abstention features no further in either version; similarly if the fideicommissary refuses he is not heard of again. So much by way of background.

II

To the text: what follows is concerned exclusively with the second part, from *aut omnimodo*. It makes the following points[114]: the property is to be sold, and the

---

[113] Jul. D37.10.7.5; Gai. D29.1.17.1; Paul D42.5.6.pr lib 58 ad edictum (where the last phrase suggests a system of *bonorum distractio* rather than *venditio* which may be interpolated); Val. D36.1.69.2 lib 3 fideicommissorum (where it is plain that the words *bonis patris eius venditis* refer to the hypothesis that the *fideicommissum* has not been made over).

[114] There is a syntactical difficulty at this point in the text: how is *aut omnimodo ... to be* joined to what precedes? Since sale of the property must be presumed to proceed only if it is not accepted by the fideicommissary, the words—in spite of the *aut*—must be understood as a consequence of the refusal, and so as following from *toto discedat*. More suitable than *aut* would be *et*: we can perhaps emend. (It may be worth noting that F reads only *a,* which has by F^2 been extended to *aut*.) There does not seem to be any alternative to this grammatical construction of the text. The only other possibility which suggests itself is to take *aut omnimodo bona vendenda sunt* as intending a contrast with *optio deferenda ... ut aut ... adgnoscat aut toto discedat*. For this view the parallel between the gerundives might give some encouragement (and it would be possible to add an *aut* before *optio*). But this construction presents material difficulties: firstly, that other texts envisage *bonorum venditio* not as an alternative to offering a choice but as the consequence of making a particular choice; secondly, that the last sentence with its *in potestate illius* is false if sale is envisaged as an alternative to giving the fideicommissary a choice.

excess restored to the pupil; if all the property cannot be sold then the fideicommissary is not to be allowed any actions: for he had the chance to take the whole and restore any excess to the pupil. If we attempt to interpret this in accordance with classical principle several problems arise. Sale of the property must indicate refusal by the fideicommissary. The main difficulties are these: (a) 'excess to the pupil': but since *bonorum venditio* is sale of the estate as a unit there can be no excess; (b) 'not all the property can be sold': similarly, under *bonorum venditio* it is impossible that all the property should not be sold[115]; (c) if the fideicommissary has refused, why should it be necessary to deny him any actions?; (d) if the fideicommissary has accepted, why should he have to restore the excess (what excess?) to the pupil?

The conclusion seems inescapable that Scaevola is not dealing here with the classical system of *bonorum venditio*. It is worth considering whether the text may refer to *bonorum distractio,* a system in which the estate was not sold as a unit, but articles belonging to it were sold as required to satisfy individual creditors. This system, late-classical and at first restricted to certain circumstances[116], offered the advantage that not all the property was at once sold up. Views divide on the question whether *bonorum distractio* was available in the case that it was abstention by a pupil which caused the need to sell the estate[117]. Without venturing into that question, we can first review what difference the hypothesis of *bonorum distractio* would make to Scaevola's case. Difficulty (a) can be disposed of, since it is now possible that after all creditors have been satisfied some property may remain unsold. Difficulties (c) and (d) are unaffected. Difficulty (b) is transformed: 'not all the property can be sold' reads strangely in conjunction with *bonorum distractio*, a system whose very object and advantage it was that not all the property need be sold. So whichever system of execution is posited, the words *si in solidum bona venire non possunt* remain incomprehensible. There seems no alternative to expunging them as a maladroit gloss[118].

Further difficulties remain, and may be considered for both systems of execution. First, *bonorum venditio*. As already stated, no excess could occur. Consequently the deletion of the words *ut ... servetur*[119] and *et ... servare* is also necessary. The following remains:

(Version 1) <et>[120] [aut] omnimodo bona vendenda sunt et omnimodo actiones fideicommissario denegandae erunt: erat enim in potestate illius universum suscipere.

---

[115] Somebody would surely enter a bid at the very lowest level.

[116] E.g. the case of the *furiosus:* Ulp. D42.4.7.10 lib 59 ad edictum.

[117] For the literature, see note 124.

[118] However one tries to interpret the words (*et si* ,even if'; *etsi,* although) they bring no sense for either system of sale of property.

[119] The words *id quod superfluum est* were already suspected by *W. Kalb,* Roms Juristen nach ihrer Sprache dargestellt (1890) 22, although he makes the extraordinary statement that they are 'sachlich nicht anzufechten'.

[120] See note 114.

This is if not laudable at least intelligible, although the force of *omnimodo* is obscure[121], and the statement that the fideicommissary is to be denied actions is after his refusal of the estate banal[122]. Yet there is nothing positively wrong with what is left of the text, unless *actiones ... denegandae* is taken to be a strict reference to *denegatio actionis*—for that surely cannot have taken place, since the fideicommissary can hardly have attempted to bring the actions he had refused to inherit[123]. There is at any rate a certain internal connexion between the phrases, for if we reject one, more must follow: if the reference to *denegatio actionis* is found offensive, and the words added to those in post-classical quarantine, then the 'Begründung' *erat enim ... suscipere* must follow; if *omnimodo* is dispatched then not much is left:

> (Version 2) <et> [aut] bona vendenda sunt.

This at least can be defended as an unassailably classical position. The choice therefore is between retaining the text less three glosses (version 1) and retaining only the first few words (version 2). While the grounds for cutting the sympathetic version 1 down to the drastic version 2 are not all compelling, there are some points in favour of the second version, notably that there is plainly a good deal wrong with the text anyway, and the words dealing with denial of actions are at best pointless, possibly incorrect.

Second, what difference does it make if we suppose that the text is concerned with *bonorum distractio*? Since the sale is not of the estate as a unit, there may be an excess; since there is no universal successor, it seems fair enough that the *curator bonorum* should make it over to the pupil. The words *ut ... servetur* may therefore be retained in this version. The same however cannot be said for the second reference to an excess, since it is impossible to see why the fideicommissary should, after the pupil's abstention, be required to make over the 'excess' (however that is to be understood) to him. This version therefore also requires the deletion of *et ... servare*.

> (Version 3) <et> [aut] omnimodo bona vendenda sunt ut id quod superfluum est pupillo servetur et omnimodo actiones fideicommissario denegandae erunt: erat enim in potestate illius universum suscipere.

For the sake of completeness here is a fourth version, produced on the same arguments as version 2, except for *bonorum distractio:*

> (Version 4) <et> [aut] bona vendenda sunt ut id quod superfluum est pupillo servetur.

---

[121] Both are glosses, according to VIR s.h.v.

[122] The plural indicates that it is actions of the estate that are in question, rather than the fideicommissary's single action for an undivided share of the estate.

[123] But see A. Metro, BIDR 75 (1972) 133-149 who argues that *denegatio actionis* in the context of *fideicommissa* is not always to be taken literally, but as meaning simply that there is no action available.

It is evident from this discussion that the question which system of execution is behind the text makes little difference to the scale of textual disturbance that we are forced to suppose. It is not possible here to examine the evidence and arguments on either side fully. In my view however the balance of the evidence suggests that the classical jurists would not have considered *bonorum distractio* in this case[124]. For this view the text of Scaevola offers some support. Although one of the references to *bonorum distractio* may be defensible, the context of the other, at the end of the text, marks the addition as certain. If a classical reconstruction of the text must then deal with *bonorum venditio*, which version is to be preferred? This is hardly to be decided with certainty. But studying an individual juristic work has some advantages. Most notably, the opportunity to use clear cases to form an impression of the general process of revision and alteration to which a work has been subject, and so to produce a measure (albeit subjective) for use in hard cases. It is plain that some texts of the LSQPT have been extensively reworked, and on this measure even the drastic textual reconstruction (version 2) may not seen implausible.

9. Pal.191: D42.8.24 [125]

Pupillus patri heres extitit et uni creditorum solvit: mox abstinuit hereditate paterna: bona patris veneunt: an id quod accepit creditor revocandum sit ne melioris condicionis sit quam ceteri creditores? an distinguimus per gratificationem acceperit an non, ut si per gratificationem tutorum revocetur ad eandem portionem quam ceteri creditores fuerint laturi: sin vero iuste exegerit, ceteri creditores neglexerint exactionem, interea res deterior facta sit vel mortalitate *vel subductis rebus mobilibus vel rebus soli ad irritum perductis, id quod acceperit creditor revocari nullo pacto **potest, quoniam alii creditores suae neglegentiae expensum ferre debeant. quid ergo si cum in eo +essent ut bona debitoris mei venirent, solverit mihi pecuniam: an actione revocari ea possit a me? an distinguendum est is optulerit mihi an ego illi extorserim invito, et si extorserim invito revocetur, si non extorserim non revocetur? sed vigilavi, meliorem meam condicionem feci, ius civile vigilantibus scriptum est: ideoque non revocatur id quod percepi.

*vel *del. Mo.*   **potest] possit *Mo.*
+essent] esset *Hal.*

---

[124] The clearest discussions of this problem are found in *S. Solazzi*, BIDR 16 (1904) 89-123 and *C. Cosentini*, SDHI 11 (1945) 1-18. *Cosentini's* arguments against *Solazzi's* view that following on abstention *bonorum distractio* would be the method of sale seem to me convincing. Together with Scaevola's text therefore, Paul D42.5.6pr must be regarded as interpolated.

[125] Translation: A pupil became heir to his father and paid off one of the creditors; he then abstained from his father's estate and the property was sold up. Should the payment received by the creditor be reclaimed so that his position is no better than that of the other creditors? Should we distinguish according to whether he received payment through special favour or not, so that if the payment was through the tutors' special favour it may be reduced to the same portion that other creditors will receive; yet if he has rightly demanded payment while the other creditors have neglected to exact it, and in the meantime the property has deteriorated either by the perishing of moveable goods or the reduction of land to infertility, what the creditor received can in no way be reclaimed, since the other creditors should pay the price of their own

II. Analysis

I

The fragment deals with two problems. For the time being we shall discuss only the first (up to *ferre debeant*). In it a pupil has become heir to his father and paid off one of his father's creditors. He has then abstained from the estate, which as a consequence has been sold. The question is whether the payment should be revoked, so that that creditor is not unduly privileged with respect to other creditors. Scaevola goes on to ask whether the issue of revocability of the payment should be decided according to whether the payment was made through special favour.

Two questions arise. First, in what circumstances might a payment to a creditor before abstention be valid? Here the point of time, the position of other creditors, and the stimulus to pay must be examined. Second, if appropriate how would the payment be revoked? It is easiest to consider the second question first, to provide the context in which the first question must be seen[126]. The text is in the title *quae in fraudem creditorum facta sunt ut restituantur*; the most obvious place to begin is therefore with the fraudulent remedies: the *restitutio in integrum* for fraudulent acts[127], and the *interdictum fraudatorium*[128]. Both remedies were available in similar circumstances, the restitution to the *curator bonorum* against acts undertaken fraudulently by the debtor with a person who had knowledge of the fraud (*qui fraudem non ignoraverit* in the wording of the edict); the interdict to any creditor put at a disadvantage by fraudulent acts, against any acquirer with knowledge of the fraud (*sciente te* in the edict). Both remedies depended therefore on fraudulent conduct by the debtor, and knowledge on the part of the acquirer: bad faith, in other words, on both sides.

Are these elements in Scaevola's text? It makes the following points about revocation: (1) 'that one creditor should not be in a better position than the others'. This is an appeal purely to fairness and even-handedness. But this is a different matter from fraud, since unequal treatment may be meted out without the presence of any bad faith. To aim for equal treatment is to aim much higher than to aim to stamp out fraud. (2) *per gratificationem*. A payment made through special favour is to be revoked. Yet there is a borderline (if sometimes nebulous) between favour and fraud. If we are to see fraud in *gratificatio* then we shall have

---

negligence. But what if my debtor has paid me money when matters were in such a position that the property was being sold up? Can it be reclaimed from me by an action? Must we distinguish whether he offered it to me or I extorted it from him against his will; so that if I extorted it, it may be reclaimed, while if I did not it may not? But I was vigilant and improved my own position. The civil law is written for the vigilant: so what I received is not reclaimed.

[126] *A priori* neither a *vindicatio* can be expected, since the payee will have become *dominus*, nor a *condictio indebiti*, since it is not true to say that the sum was not owed.

[127] *Lenel*, EP 435-.

[128] *Lenel*, EP 495-; *Kaser*, RP I 252.

to read into the word not only bad faith and intention to defraud on the part of the debtor, but also bad faith on the part of the creditor. But this is a bold move[129].

So far there is not much reason to suppose that the text is concerned with the revocation of fraudulent acts. Before going further, another text may be examined[130]:

> Paul D42.5.6.2 lib 58 ad edictum. Quid ergo si quibusdam creditoribus solvit, deinde bona venierint? si quaeratur an repetitio sit, ex causa id statuendum Iulianus ait, ne alterius aut neglegentia aut cupiditas huic qui diligens fuit noceat. quod si utroque instante tibi gratificatus tutor solvit, aequum esse aut prius eandem portionem mihi quaeri aut communicandum quod accepisti: et hoc Iulianus ait. apparet autem loqui eum si ex bonis paternis solutum sit. quid ergo si aliunde pupillus solverit? reddi ei debebit nec ne? et utrum a creditore an ex hereditate? Scaevola noster ait, si aliquid sit in bonis, deducendum ex hereditate solidum, exemplo eius qui gessit negotia: sed si nihil sit in bonis non esse iniquum adversus creditorem dandam repetitionem quasi indebiti soluti.

This text too (as the *principium* and §1 show) deals with a pupil. For the moment, we go no further than *et hoc Iulianus ait*[131]. Up to that point the following is outlined: a pupil has become heir and paid certain creditors; as a result of his abstention the estate has then been sold, and the question of revocability of the payments has arisen. Julian was of the view that the question must be decided according to the circumstances, so that negligence or greed should not play a role; he also said that if two creditors were equally persistent, and the tutor favoured one and paid him, then the other should also have been paid the same, or obtain his share of what was paid to the favourite.

The similarity in language and content in this text and Scaevola is most remarkable (*gratificatus* and its cognates are rare). Paul is a little more precise, since he notes that special favour was shown to one when another was also pressing his claim (*utroque instante*); this clarification of *gratificatio* is not found in Scaevola. Yet Paul's text is not wholly unobjectionable: the words *ne alterius*

---

[129] All one can expect is that *gratificatio* means that the debtor was in bad faith in employing special favour. Reading more into the word is dangerous; the more so as it appears in only one other text, Scaev. D11.7.46pr lib 2 quaestionum, in an entirely different, obscure and suspect context (*Beseler*, SZ 66 [1948] 308).

[130] Translation: But what if he pays certain creditors and then the property is sold up? If it should be asked whether there is a reclaim, Julian says that this must be determined according to the circumstances, so that the negligence or greed of one should not harm a diligent person. But if when both creditors have been pressing for payment, the tutor has paid you through favour, it is fair that I should already have received the same portion or that you should share with me what you have received: this is what Julian says. Yet he appears to be referring to payment from the father's estate. But what if the pupil has paid from elsewhere? Will the payment have to be returned or not? And if so, from the creditor or the estate? Scaevola says that if the estate is solvent the full sum is to be deducted from it on the analogy of *negotiorum gestio*. But if the estate is insolvent it is not unjust to give against the creditor a reclaim as if for payment of money not owed.

[131] The words *apparet* ... are concerned with the source of the payment by the pupil. They are not relevant at this point but are discussed below.

... *noceat* are not illuminating: how is the carelessness of one creditor (that is, his slowness in pressing a claim) supposed to harm another? How is the greed of one supposed to prejudice another who was diligently looking after his own interests? How does one distinguish between greed and diligence? The words are best eliminated [132]. Similarly there is some difficulty in understanding how it is possible that one creditor should have been paid through special favour, yet another may already have received the same (apparently not through special favour).

For all this, the text does raise the issue of *gratificatio* in a reasonably clear way: the view that a preferential payment to one creditor, when another is also bringing a claim, should not be upheld seems appropriate. This brings us back to a point already made: where other things are equal one creditor should not obtain a *melior condicio* than another, yet this is a more ambitious aim than the curbing and revocation of fraudulent acts. Since both Scaevola and Paul fail to give an indication that fraud has been committed, another remedy may be sought.

II

It is worth attempting to understand the text in close relation to the *ius abstinendi* with which it begins. It was pointed out during the discussion of Pal.190 that the praetor did allow a pupil (but not normally a *pubes*) to abstain from an estate even after meddling with it [133]. The pupil remained heir but no actions were permitted against him. For a *pubes* on the other hand the matter is straightforward: if he interfered with the estate he lost the right to abstain from it. Since this was not the case for a pupil, the question arises what the status of the actions taken by him in relation to the estate prior to his abstention was after it. On this point there are several texts to consider:

(1) Jul. D29.2.44 lib 47 digestorum [134]. Quotiens pupillus patri heres exstitit et abstinet se hereditate, quamvis patris bona sub creditoribus fiant, tamen rata haberi debent quaecumque pupillus bona fide gesserit: et ideo ei qui fundum tutore auctore a pupillo emerit succurrendum erit: nec interest pupillus solvendo sit nec ne.

Actions taken by the pupil in good faith ought to be held valid: this is stated as a principle, and then applied to the case of a buyer of land from the pupil (with tutor's authorisation). He must be aided (*succurrendum*) whether the pupil is

---

[132] Cf. *W. Kunkel,* SZ 45 (1925) 323, whose verdict ('vielleicht nachklassischer Herkunft') is more cautious.

[133] Gai. D29.2.57pr lib 23 ad edictum provinciale.

[134] Translation: Whenever a pupil becomes heir to his father and abstains from the estate, although the father's property is sold up by the creditors, nonetheless whatever the pupil has done in good faith should be ratified. And so the buyer of land from the pupil on his tutor's authority must be aided, whether the pupil is solvent or not.

solvent or not. The buyer's possession is unassailable, as the statement that the pupil's insolvency is irrelevant makes clear. But what is the protection? *Succurrendum* must refer here, as often, to a praetorian remedy[135]. It is evidently a remedy against an action which could otherwise be brought against the buyer by the creditors, that is necessarily a real action. We cannot however suppose that on sale by the pupil (which was with tutor's authorisation) the buyer failed to become *dominus*. Consequently we must suppose that the abstention by the pupil cast some doubt on the status of his actions with regard to the estate[136]. That some process of review of his actions was made is supported also by the use of the word *rata*; and since this sale is held to be valid, praetorian protection is made available. But the need to specify that this action was ratified indicates that others might not pass through the net[137]. If an action was not approved, praetorian protection would be declined, and there would be no obstacle to the creditors' real action.

(2) Paul D42.5.6.1 lib 58 ad edictum[138]. Si pupillus antequam abstineret aliquid gesserit, servandum est utique si bona fide gessit.

Julian's principle that actions taken in good faith are to be held valid (*servandum*) is repeated. Details lack, but the contrary argument is obvious: an act taken in bad faith would somehow be revoked.

If we return now to the text of Scaevola and the similar one of Paul cited earlier, then the reference to *gratificatio* in both can be understood as a question whether the payments made by the pupil were in good faith. Since acts not taken in good faith could not be ratified, it was worth considering whether special favour towards a debtor could be regarded as impugning his good faith and so as vitiating the payment.

If the remedy here was not the *interdictum fraudatorium*, what was it? Some texts appear to refer to a *condictio indebiti*. (a) Paul D42.5.6.2 (cited above) does towards the end. The question it raises there, however, is different: the father's

---

[135] *Heumann-Seckel*, s.v. *succurro*. It is common for *in integrum restitutiones*, but is also used for the granting of *exceptiones*.

[136] Unless one were to suppose that the pupil had requested a *spatium deliberandi*. This, although introduced for the benefit of *heredes extranei* before making *aditio*, was nonetheless extended in late classical law to the case of *sui* considering abstention. A text of Ulpian makes it clear that a pupil would need to present a *iusta causa* in order to proceed to an alienation during a period of deliberation (Ulp. D28.8.7pr- lib 60 ad edictum). It is hard to see that sale of land would count, since the *iustae causae* enumerated in D28.8.7.3 concern burial, urgent repairs or cultivation or the avoidance of penalties or sale of pledges in connexion with debts owed. The prohibition on alienation had real effect (Pomp. D18.1.26 lib 17 ad Sabinum) so the buyer did not become *dominus*.

[137] It is as well to emphasise that the suggestion here is not that the praetor reconsidered the acts taken on his own initiative; rather he would wait for an application from an interested party, in this case the creditors seeking revocation.

[138] Translation: If a pupil has taken any action prior to abstaining, it must be upheld provided it was taken in good faith.

debt has been paid from the pupil's resources. Here it can be understood that the payment could be regarded as undue, and reclaim permitted. The use of *quasi* to indicate that this would be an unusual application of the *condictio indebiti* might just redeem the text as classical. (b) another text of Scaevola[139]:

> Scaev. D12.6.61 lib 5 responsorum. Tutores pupilli quibusdam creditoribus patris ex patrimonio paterno solverunt, sed postea non sufficientibus bonis pupillum abstinuerunt: quaeritur an quod amplius creditoribus per tutores pupilli solutum est vel totum quod acceperunt restituere debeant. respondi, si nihil dolo factum esset, tutori quidem vel pupillo non deberi, creditoribus autem aliis in id quod amplius sui debiti solutum est teneri.

The facts of the case are extremely similar to those of D42.8.24: should creditors paid before abstention have to repay the whole or part of what they received? The *responsum* is that provided *dolus* was not involved the creditors are not liable to the pupil or his tutor, but to repay the excess they received to the other creditors. The text is not free from objections: *quod amplius* the creditors have received is vague: more than what? Liability to repay *id quod amplius sui debiti solutum est* is extraordinary, since we can scarcely suppose that they were paid more than was owed to them. It is of course clear that both these comparatives are intended to refer to 'more' than the dividend which creditors would receive from the *bonorum emptor*. But the fact that the language is so imprecise raises suspicion. It is hard too to make much sense of the statement that the 'prepaid' creditors are not liable to the pupil or his tutor. Why should they be? The words *tutori ... deberi* can be deleted without disturbing the structure of the sentence and are probably a gloss. The compilers placed this fragment in the title *de condictione indebiti*. That is in itself most remarkable, for the creditors of the pupil's father are being paid from the father's estate. I do not think we can suppose that classical law would have admitted a *condictio indebiti* in such circumstances. The context of the fragment has therefore been changed, a change which helps to explain the words *amplius sui debiti*, words which while factually incorrect help to ground the idea that the payment was not due and that the *condictio indebiti* might be used to recover it. The words are likely to be interpolated[140]. Yet disposal of them forces also the removal of the reference to *dolus*, since otherwise we are left with a *responsum* which reads *respondi si nihil*

---

[139] Translation: A pupil's tutors paid certain creditors of his father from the father's estate, but later when the estate proved insolvent abstained the pupil from it: the question is whether those creditors should return the excess paid to them by the pupil's tutors or all that they received. I replied, that if no fraud was involved, there was no liability to the tutor or pupil, but there was to the other creditors for the amount paid in excess of what was owed to them.

[140] To whom is the interpolation to be attributed? If we can reckon on some degree of consistency within the compilation then the interpolation is probably not compilatorial: the *condictio indebiti* had not been adopted as the general remedy for reclaim of an excessive share from 'pre-paid' creditors. (Had it been then D42.8.24 would surely also refer to it.) It is more likely that the reference to a *condictio indebiti* was found already in the text by the compilers, and that it was on that basis that they assigned it to title D12.6. The origin is therefore most likely post-classical.

dolo factum esset creditoribus aliis teneri, and the exclusion of liability in the case of *dolus* is absurd. The motive for the introduction of *dolus* is however clear: when the text was altered to refer to the *condictio indebiti* it was desirable to make it clear that there was a liability to repay even if no *dolus* was present (in the case of *dolus* the *actio doli* or *interdictum fraudatorium* could be made available).

What then would the original text have stated? Since there is no reference to the payments having been fraudulent or dolose, we may exclude the interdict on fraud and continue the search for other remedies not only for D42.8.24, but for the case in D12.6.61 as well.

There are very few options. The best seems to be to suppose that an *in integrum restitutio* could be given after abstention to undo the effects of actions which after abstention there was no particular reason to hold to be valid[141]. This restitution is to be distinguished sharply from that made available against acts *fraudationis causa*. The texts give some ground (other than the need to find a remedy in cases where others are plainly not available) to believe in the existence of such an *in integrum restitutio*. Two of the relevant texts have already been considered: (1) Jul. D29.2.44: *bona fide* acts are to be ratified; they are ratified in the sense that they are not subject to revocation through *in integrum restitutio*; (2) Paul D42.5.6.2 suggests a similar situation; (3) Pap. D4.4.31 lib 9 responsorum[142]:

Si mulier postquam heres extitit propter aetatem abstinendi causa in integrum restituta fuerit, servos hereditarios ex fideicommisso ab ea recte manumissos retinere libertatem respondi: nec erunt cogendi viginti aureos pro libertate retinenda dependere quam iure optimo consecuti videntur. nam et si quidam ex creditoribus pecuniam suam ante restitutionem ab ea reciperassent, ceterorum querella contra eos qui acceperunt ut pecunia communicetur non admittetur.

This text deals with a woman who is not a pupil but a minor and has through *in integrum restitutio* been permitted to abstain from the estate. In the second part of the text (which alone concerns us here), some creditors have been paid before the abstention. Other, unpaid, creditors attempt to claim a share in those payments, but their attempt is turned down. We are not told that they attempted to bring a remedy for fraud, and that it was refused as the woman's actions were not fraudulent. Rather we must suppose that their claim was based on the argument that since the heir had abstained there was no reason why her actions

---

[141] S. Solazzi, La revoca degli atti fraudolenti³ (Naples, 1945) II 133n1. In his third edition Solazzi rightly withdraws his earlier statement that D29.2.44, D42.5.6.2, and D.4.4.31 refer to the *interdictum utile* for fraud mentioned in Ulp. D42.8.10.10 lib 73 ad edictum. Since that interdict also required the alienator to have intention to defraud, it is no more applicable to these cases (in which fraudulent intention is not mentioned) than the other remedies for fraud. An *in integrum restitutio*, although not the one *fraudationis causa*, is altogether more probable.

[142] Translation: If a woman after becoming heir has on account of her age obtained *in integrum restitutio* in order to abstain, I replied that slaves belonging to the estate who had been properly manumitted by her in accordance with a *fideicommissum* retain their freedom: nor will they be compelled to pay twenty *aurei* for retaining it, since they had a good entitlement to it. For even if certain creditors had received their money before restitution, a claim by other creditors against them that the money received should be shared would not be admitted.

in paying some creditors should retain validity[143]. Papinian too appears to have taken the view that actions taken in good faith should not be revoked.

These three texts are all also cited by *Solazzi* in support of the view that there was an *in integrum restitutio* based on the objective fact of the abstention of an heir, and applicable to actions which had not been taken in good faith[144]. A further piece of evidence can be added, from Ulpian's discussion of the edictal clause *si suus heres erit* in book 61 of his edictal commentary[145]:

> D29.2.71.3-4. Praetor ait 'si per eum eamve factum erit, quo quid ex ea hereditate amoveretur'. (4) Si quis suus se dicit retinere hereditatem nolle, aliquid autem ex hereditate amoverit, abstinendi beneficium non habebit.
>
> D29.2.71.9. Haec verba edicti ad eum pertinent qui ante quid amovit deinde se abstinet: ceterum si ante se abstinuit deinde tunc amovit, hic videamus an edicto locus sit. magisque est ut putem istic Sabini sententiam admittendam, scilicet ut furti potius actione creditoribus teneatur: etenim qui semel se abstinuit quemadmodum ex post delicto obligatur?

The edictal quotation is unfortunately incomplete since §3 does not give us the consequences of *amovere*. §§ 5 to 8 discuss details of the wording which are of no concern here. There is an apparent contradiction in the discussion: §4 states that an *amovere* results in loss of the power to abstain, while §9 specifically speaks of *qui ante quid amovit, deinde se abstinet*; indeed §9 explicitly limits the application of the edict to that case, an *amovere* subsequent to abstention being treated as theft[146]. The conclusion is therefore necessary that the generalisation in §4 be limited so that not every *amovere* results in loss of the power to abstain. §3 after all does not state that 'if through him or her some object should be caused to be removed from the estate, then he or she shall forfeit the power to abstain'. What it did state remains unclear. But an attempt at reconstruction may be made. It is well known that the praetor distinguished between *pubes* and *impubes* in the edict *si suus heres erit*; and it is the same distinction which must be employed here. An *amovere* constitutes an *immiscere* in the estate which will cause a *pubes* to lose his power to abstain. There is no need for the *amovere* to be made further punishable, for the loss of the ability to abstain brings with it the unavoidable need to deal with the consequences of the *amovere*. For the *pubes* therefore, there

---

[143] Cf. *Solazzi*, revoca II 134.

[144] *Solazzi*, revoca II 133n1.

[145] *Lenel*, EP 418-. The clause *si suus heres erit* is the equivalent for *sui* of the clause *cui heres non extabit* for *extranei* (*Lenel* 416). Translation: (3) The praetor says 'if through him or her it should have been brought about that something has been removed from this estate'. (4) If a *suus heres* says he does not want to retain an estate, but has removed something from it, he will not have the privilege of abstaining. (9) These words in the edict apply to a person who has first removed something and then abstains: but if he has first abstained and then removed something, let us see whether the edict is applicable. And it is better, I should think, to accept the view of Sabinus, which is that he is liable to the creditors in an action for theft: [as when someone has once abstained, how is he later obliged by delict?]

[146] In §9 *etenim ... obligatur* must be interpolated: *Beseler*, SZ 51 (1931) 73.

is no real need to distinguish between *amovere* and *immiscere*. All this is different where pupils are involved: they do not lose their ability to abstain if they meddle with the estate. Should they lose it if they perform an *amovere*? §9 makes it plain that they do not: how else to explain *amovere* followed by abstention? Yet *amovere* cannot be allowed to remain unchecked. What distinguishes *amovere* from *immiscere* is the bad faith involved in the former[147]. An *amovere* calls into operation the edictal clause cited in §3. Its effect is not that the pupil is prevented from abstaining, but that an act taken in bad faith is on the basis of this edict revoked.

It may be useful to recapitulate the differences between the facts required for the proposed *in integrum restitutio* and the one available *fraudationis causa*: (1) the restitution in the case of fraud is available (a) if the alienator is in bad faith and (b) intending to defraud, and (c) the recipient is in bad faith; (2) the restitution in case of abstention is available (a) following abstention by the heir (b) if he has alienated in bad faith.

III

If it is accepted that the first part of the present text originally referred to an *in integrum restitutio* dependent on the objective fact of abstention, applicable to acts taken in bad faith, and promulgated in the edict *si suus heres erit*, then it remains to consider other points raised in the text. These are, firstly, the distinction made between payment received *per gratificationem* and other payment, and, secondly, the reference to the negligence of other creditors and the decline in the value of the estate.

First, *gratificatio*. The distinction made here has been suspected since *Faber* as a Tribonian import[148]. Yet if we accept the view of Julian cited by Paul, then the question whether the payment was made through special favour or not is important so that the question whether it was *bona fide* can be answered; and on that question the revocability or not of the payment depends.

A distinction may therefore be of some value. But the distinction in Scaevola is extremely strange. A contrast appears to be intended between the case where the creditor received payment through special favour and the case where he rightly demanded payment. Yet one may have a just entitlement and still have it satisfied owing to special favour. While the mention of *gratificatio* may then be relevant to

---

[147] D29.2.71.8: *amovere non videtur qui non callido animo nec maligno rem seposuit* (reading with *Mommsen* in place of *reposuit, seposuit*).

[148] Coniecturae 20.14.14: 'nam et ei [Triboniano] familiarius est distinguere ac subdistinguere quam Scaevolae (cuius responsa unico ut plurimum verbo concluduntur).' This is of course correct, but it is as well to remember that we are dealing here not with a *responsum* but a *quaestio*. The stylistic differences between the two genres are extremely marked in Scaevola.

the question of revocability, the form in which it is raised is suspicious (the more so as it is so similar to the second distinction in the text, which is itself dubious—see below; and because in the end no consequences are drawn from it).

Second, negligence and deterioration. It is in the second part of the distinction that the references to negligence and deterioration are introduced. These have been suspected as interpolations[149]; and certainly from a formal point of view there is a good deal that is offensive in the rambling asyndeton in which the supposed contrast is expanded from just exaction to incorporate negligence by the other creditors coupled with the decline in the value of the property.

The reference to deterioration is superfluous. The fact that the pupil has abstained casts already a troubled shadow over the solvency of the estate. So if a creditor has been paid in full beforehand then his position is bound to be better than that of other creditors (unless they can obtain revocation of the payment) even if the value of the estate does not decline. In other texts the reference to deterioration can be justified[150]. Here, introduced as an additional circumstance, it is hard to defend, and the fact that it appears not to be an integral part of the contrast but instead to be tacked on must raise suspicion that it is a gloss.

As for negligence, it is not so clearly out of place as in Paul D42.5.6.2 (glossed). It could be seen as a contrast with *gratificatio*, in which, as the text of Paul (D42.5.6.2) illustrates, the idea is of more than one entitled creditor pursuing a claim, but only one being satisfied, through favour. Contrast the case of negligence, where the other creditors do not get around to bringing their claims. Yet the assumptions underlying this mention of negligence are curious. Particularly odd is the supposition that all creditors must have been entitled to claim at the same time but some did not trouble to do so. Further, *neglegentia* as a reason for refusing revocation is entirely inappropriate, for it is not for that reason but because payment of a due debt was made in good faith that the revocation of a payment can be denied. It seems necessary therefore to regard *quoniam ... debeant* as a gloss. Whether *ceteri creditores neglexerint exactionem* should also be discarded is less clear.

IV

So much for the first part of the text. But there is a second (from *quid ergo* ...), and a new range of problems. Here the question is whether, when a debtor about to undergo *bonorum venditio* has repaid me (one of his creditors), the payment is

---

[149] *Kunkel*, SZ 45 (1925) 326.

[150] Ulp. D42.4.8 and D28.8.7.3 lib 60 ad edictum; Ulp. D28.8.5.1 lib 70 (read 60? *Cujas*) ad edictum. All of these texts deal with the *ius deliberandi*. So there is for the time being no heir, but it is desirable that action should be taken to limit loss caused to the *hereditas iacens* by perishable property left unattended. In these cases it is precisely the possibility of deterioration which justifies the praetor in granting the (not yet) heir the power to intervene.

revocable. Again the text enquires whether it is necessary to make a distinction, but this time the one suggested is different: is it important to distinguish between the case where the debtor freely offers to pay (in which case there is to be no revocation) and the case where the creditor extorts payment from him (in which case the payment can be revoked)? There follows a statement that I (the creditor) was vigilant and improved my position; the famous maxim *ius civile vigilantibus scriptum est*; and the answer that there is to be no revocation.

How much this problem has in common with the first is unclear. Plainly, *bonorum venditio* and payment to a creditor[151]. But beyond that it is not easy to go: is it to be supposed that the sale follows on abstention by a pupil? There seems to be a clear break in the text at *quid ergo,* and the creditor is suddenly transformed into 'me'. This being so, and there being no indication that the text is concerned with the sale of an abandoned estate rather than with the sale of a debtor's property *inter vivos*, let alone with pupils or abstention, it is as well to interpret the problem if possible without relying on them.

Two other texts from the same title are important. Both are from Ulpian, and in both Julian is cited[152]:

Ulp. D42.8.6.7 lib 66 ad edictum. Sciendum Iulianum scribere eoque iure nos uti ut qui debitam pecuniam recepit ante quam bona debitoris possideantur, quamvis sciens prudensque solvendo non esse recipiat, non timere hoc edictum: sibi enim vigilavit. qui vero post bona possessa debitum suum recepit, hunc in portionem vocandum exaequandumque ceteris creditoribus: neque enim debuit praeripere ceteris post bona possessa, cum iam par condicio omnium creditorum facta esset.

Ulp. D42.8.10.16 lib 73 ad edictum. Si debitorem meum et complurium creditorum consecutus essem fugientem secum ferentem pecuniam et abstulissem ei id quod mihi debeatur, placet Iuliani sententia dicentis multum interesse, antequam in possessionem bonorum eius creditores mittantur hoc factum sit an postea: si ante, cessare in factum actionem, si postea, huic locum fore.

Similarities between these two texts are obvious, and it is likely that in writing them Ulpian had the same discussion of Julian in mind. That however is not material here. In both a clear distinction is drawn: a payment of due money to a creditor before the creditors have been *missi in bona* is valid and the creditor cannot be called on to repay. But payment after *missio in bona* is not admissible.

---

[151] *Solazzi,* revoca II 132 argues that it deals with payment to any creditor by any debtor.

[152] Translation: (6.7) Julian writes, and this is the law we use, that someone who has received money owed to him before possession has been taken of a debtor's property, even in full knowledge of the debtor's insolvency, need not fear this edict: for he was looking after his own interests. But someone who has received his due after the property has been taken into possession must be called to account and reduced to the same share as the other creditors: for he ought not to seize an advantage over the others after the taking of possession, since the condition of all creditors has then been made equal. (10.16) If I pursued a debtor of mine and of other creditors while he was fleeing and carrying money and took from him what he owed me, Julian's view is accepted, which is that it makes a great difference whether this is done before the creditors are sent into possession of his property or after: if before, the action is not available; if after, it is.

To use Julian's terminology, the first of these demonstrates vigilance but the second fraud: receipt beforehand even in the knowledge that the debtor is incapable of meeting all his liabilities shows vigilance; but receipt afterwards when the condition of all creditors should be equal gives rise to the *interdictum fraudatorium*[153]. One point is stressed: the timing of the payment.

To return to Scaevola. The most obvious point which arises from looking at Ulpian's discussion is that in Scaevola the timing is most unclear. Far from being treated as the decisive criterion, it is abandoned to obscurity so that it is not even clear whether *missio in bona* has taken place[154]. Instead of timing, Scaevola's text concentrates on a quite different question: was the payment voluntary or enforced? It is unfortunate that the state of textual evidence does not allow us to quantify the degree of force involved in Scaevola's term *extorserim*, compared with Ulpian's description of the tactless but effective conduct of the creditor in D42.8.10.16 (*consecutus essem ... abstulissem*). In neither case is a reference made to quasi-delictual consequences; yet if no reference to *metus* is intended by Scaevola then it is hard to see what value can be attributed to his distinction between voluntary and enforced payment.

Suppose that we are dealing, as in Ulpian's cases, with fraud. Then the Scaevolan distinction is surprising. For it suggests that there should be revocation of the payment in the case of extortion but not if payment is voluntary. But the remedies for fraud require that the payer should be in bad faith and have fraudulent intentions. If however the payment was extorted from him, this cannot be said to be the case, and so revocation on ground of fraud ought not to be possible.

Vigilance is another odd matter. The parallel case (Ulp. D42.8.6.7) associates it with receipt of payment prior to *missio in bona*, but the fact that in the text of Scaevola the references to timing are lacking makes the point of referring to vigilance obscure. It follows on the distinction between voluntary and enforced payment; it is stated that in the case of vigilance there is to be no repayment, and similarly we are told that in the case of voluntary payment there is to be no repayment. But if the payment was voluntary, how can the creditor be said to have been vigilant? And if it was extorted, how can he be said not to have been vigilant?

---

[153] The reference to an *actio in factum* is a compilatorial interpolation which refers to the *actio Pauliana*. This is a standard interpolation in this title. See RE suppl. XII.1008-1019 (Impallomeni) with literature.

[154] It need not be thought that after *missio* the debtor would, on purely practical grounds, be unable to pay: *missio* did not transfer possession of the debtor's property but gave only a right to take it (Paul D41.2.3.23 lib 54 ad edictum). We are told in the text that *bonorum venditio* is about to take place, but G3.79 states that it can follow only forty days after *missio* in the case of a living person or twenty days in the case of selling up an estate (although the figures in Gaius are somewhat corrupt, that does not affect the present argument). The events in the Scaevolan text could well take place within this period, so that the debtor's practical powers over his property would remain intact. But we are not told.

To sum up. The mention of extortion fits badly with what precedes, no better with what follows. It does not seem to refer to *metus*. It does not seem to have any point. The words *an distinguendum... revocetur* are therefore to be expunged[155]. Like the distinction in the first part of the text, this one too once raised is abandoned, and no conclusions are drawn from it. For vigilance the position is less clear. The reference to it has after all until now been shown only to be inconsistent with the part of the text which is to be expunged. There seem to be two options: either (1) to suppose that Scaevola's text contained a reference to vigilance and timing (that is, up to what point a demand for payment was legitimate and so irrevocable) or (2) to suppose that the reference to vigilance has also been glossed. The text must clearly be read in close conjunction with D42.8.6.7, so this choice is equivalent to deciding whether Scaevola was discussing the same problem in similar terms to those which Ulpian reports Julian as employing, or whether to a discussion of a different problem a reference to vigilance has been added, most likely with the discussion of Ulpian-Julian in mind.

How likely is it that Scaevola was discussing fraud? Nothing speaks for this except the mention of vigilance, which is not comprehensible unless it is made clear that it must take place before *missio*. What has happened to the mention of timing? We cannot suppose that it has been deleted by the compilers, who retained it in other texts[156], so it seems most probable either that it was not in the text to start with (in which case Scaevola was not discussing fraud) or else that it has been suppressed by glossed material. The question perhaps is not finally to be resolved.

Vigilance alone (and a dubious reference to it at that) can be enlisted to argue in favour of fraudulent origins for our text. The famous maxim too fits poorly: to say that the civil law is for the vigilant is not a sufficient reason for holding each and every action that a vigilant person takes to be valid. And no civil-law remedy seems to come into question here, which adds to the inappropriateness of the resounding phrase[157]. On the whole it is not likely that this irrelevant ornament featured prominently in Scaevola's argument; and since the topic of vigilance as a whole seems loosely connected with the text, it is probably glossed. If this is so, then the best explanation for it is that it is glossed from D42.8.6.7. So the glossator is a 'Juliankenner' or an 'Ulpiankenner'[158]. Owing to the gloss the

---

[155] It is worth noting that the word *extorqueo* is found 14 times in Justinian's code but never in any of his own constitutions. It points therefore in a postclassical direction.

[156] D42.8.6.7; D42.8.10.16.

[157] *Kaser*, RP I 184n32 suggests that it is to be understood in a broad sense as 'alles Juristenrecht'. But the text does not prepare the reader for this, and it does not seem very apposite here. It is sad to have to abandon this fine phrase, but not unprecedented: *D. Liebs*, Romanitas-Christianitas (ed. G. Wirth; Berlin, 1982) 292 notes with regret that the spuriousness of Ulpian's *libri 7 regularum* forces us to regard as apocryphal D1.1.10pr *iustitia est constans et perpetua voluntas ius suum cuique tribuendi.*

fragment took on the appearance of being connected with fraud, and so could be placed by the compilers in D42.8.

Very little of this second part of the text seems worthy of retention. Extortion, vigilance and the *actio in factum* must all go. Regrettably this does not leave us with a comprehensible residue. It appears that the glosses have suppressed the original text and masked its concerns.

As for the first part of the text, while there are dubious elements at least some is comprehensible: it dealt with the *in integrum restitutio* offered in case of abstention by a pupil. This part of the fragment, in dealing with some of the consequences of abstention, plainly has something in common with Pal. 190 with which perhaps it should be read closely.

10. Pal.192: D44.3.14[159]

De accessionibus possessionum nihil in perpetuum neque generaliter definire possumus: consistunt enim in sola aequitate. (1) Plane tribuuntur his qui in locum aliorum succedunt sive ex contractu sive voluntate: heredibus enim et his qui successorum loco habentur datur accessio testatoris. (2) Itaque si mihi vendideris servum, utar accessione tua. (3) Et si mihi pignori dederis et ego eandem rem alii pigneravi, meus creditor utetur accessione tui temporis tam adversus extraneum quam adversus te ipsum, quamdiu pecuniam mihi non exsolveris: nam qui me potior est, cum ego te superaturus sim, multo magis adversus te optinere debet. sed si pecuniam mihi solveris, hoc casu accessione tua non utetur. (4) Item si absente te is qui negotia tua videbatur administrare servum mihi vendiderit, tuque reversus ratum habueris, omnimodo accessione <tua> utar. (5) Item si mihi pignori dederis et convenerit nisi pecuniam solvisses licere ex pacto pignus vendere, idque vendiderim, emptori accessio tui temporis dari debebit licet invito te pignora distracta sint: iam enim illo in tempore quo contrahebas *videri concessisse venditioni si pecuniam non intulisses.

*videri concessisse] videris consensisse *Mo.*

---

[158] Which sort of 'Kenner' we suppose depends whether we imagine that Julian's original discussion was used or a citation of it in Ulpian's commentary on the edict. The point is considered in chapter III. For the idea of a 'Juliankenner' cf. *H. J. Wolff*, 'Zur Überlieferungsgeschichte von Ulpians *libri ad Sabinum*' Festschrift Schulz II (Weimar, 1951) 145-171.

[159] Translation: We cannot define anything for ever or in general about accessions of possession, for they are based only in equity. (1) Obviously they are accorded to those who succeed to the position of others either by contract or will: for the testator's accession is given to heirs and those in the position of successors. (2) So if you have sold me a slave I may use your accession. (3) And if you have given me a pledge and I have given the same thing on to someone else as a pledge, my creditor will use the accession of your time both against third parties and against you yourself, so long as you have not repaid me: for a person with a stronger claim than I have, when I have a better one than you, ought all the more to prevail against you. But if you have repaid me, he will not use your accession. (4) Equally, if in your absence the person who was administering your affairs has sold me a slave and on your return you have ratified the sale, I may in any case use your accession. (5) Likewise if you have given me a pledge and it has been agreed unless you repay me that I am allowed to sell it, and I have sold it: the buyer must be given the accession of your time, even though the pledge was sold against your will: for at the moment of contracting you are regarded as having consented to a sale if you had not repaid me my money.

Accessio is a matter of adding periods of possession. It has its uses in two main contexts in Roman law: (a) in positive prescription (*usucapio* or *longi temporis praescriptio*), where the opportunity of adding on to one's own period of possession the period of possession of one's predecessor may make the crucial difference between having reached or not having reached the time limit for acquiring by prescription; (b) in the interdict *utrubi*, where the possessor for the purposes of the interdict was the person who had possessed for the greater part of the preceding year. Here too the time which could be added by demonstrating an entitlement to *accessio* might be decisive.

This text deals with *accessio* in *utrubi*[160]. This is not because *accessio* in prescription was a later idea, although that appears to be true[161], but more decisively because §3 refers to granting it to the pledge creditor; and it is plain that there was no point in this in the case of *usucapio*, where taking possession of a pledge would constitute no *iustum initium* and consequently acquisition of ownership would never be possible[162].

Scaevola's text, after opening with the rather surprising pronouncement that there are no set rules for *accessio* (which is all a matter of equity), goes on to list and discuss various cases: succession, sale, pledge[163], sale by a *negotiorum gestor*, sale of a pledge. Since the fragment is not concerned with solving complex problems but with listing some cases where *accessio* is available, the dogmatic difficulty it offers is slight, and the main problem one of trying to establish, where sources are scarce, whether the cases it describes are novel or obvious.

The received view on *accessio* in *utrubi* is at any rate the following: that the edict specifically provided for *accessio* in the cases of sale and succession *mortis causa* (as it did also in other interdicts[164]), but that other cases were a matter for juristic interpretation[165]. This seems to have begun and become accepted early, for Gaius lists in addition to these two edictal cases *donatio* and the constitution of dowry[166]. A similar but somewhat longer list is given later by Ulpian[167].

To turn to Scaevola. A few words on each paragraph should suffice. The *principium* states that no general definition for all time can be laid down about

---

[160] The main literature on this and its relations with *accessio* in other contexts is apparently Zanzucchi, AG 72 (1904) 358- and AG 74 (1906) 3- (unfortunately not accessible to me); but see the summary and contrary argument in P. Krüger, SZ 26 (1905) 144-8; F. Magliocca, SDHI 33 (1967) 221-278.

[161] Views differ: see *Buckland,* Textbook 243; *Kaser* RP I 423n59.

[162] N. Herzen, SZ 25 (1904) 456.

[163] No other texts appear to envisage the situation of *accessio* in pledge. But (subject to the objections raised below) this does not seem problematic.

[164] So in the interdicts *de itinere actuque privato* and *de aqua cottidiana et aestiva: Lenel,* EP 478-9.

[165] *Lenel,* EP 489; *Buckland,* Textbook 734.

[166] G4.151.

[167] D41.2.13.6-11 lib 72 ad edictum.

accessio, which is a question of equity. This is curious, since even if some cases were a matter for interpretation, others were specifically set out in the edict and therefore a matter of plain fact which ought to have been mentioned[168]. In any case the classical jurists are not often much concerned with definition[169], and it is precisely towards concrete examples (from the edict, for instance) that they are more inclined. But this is not all: Scaevola himself is scarcely interested in definition. The word *definire* is found nowhere else in his works; and *generaliter* is also not found in this context otherwise[170]. So the fragment begins with a curious and inaccurate statement in uncharacteristic language.

But who might have been interested in making such a statement? The style may look like Tribonian[171]. But Justinian changed the rules for *utrubi*, counting as possessor for the purposes of the interdict the party in possession at the time of *litis contestatio*[172]. Since the need to have possessed for the greater part of the preceding year therefore disappeared, *accessio* went with it. As for prescription, by several statutes *accessio* was made available in most circumstances[173]; and since this was established by legislation, and there was no difficulty in regulating any other cases in the same way, it seems unlikely that Tribonian could have said or thought that there were no general rules on *accessio*. Instead it might have been the postclassics who found the classical circumstances in which *accessio* was granted in either prescription or *utrubi* confusing.

§ 1 goes on to say that *accessio* is given to those who succeed to the position of others either *ex contractu* or *ex voluntate*: for the testator's accession is given, it continues, to heirs and those in the position of *successores*. There is a certain discontinuity between these two clauses, for after mentioning successors on contract or will the text proceeds to speak of heirs and successors, so by implication intending universal succession.

In fact the whole conception of succession *ex contractu* is a curious one. What is the succession to? In the case of sale, plainly to ownership. But the next example is pledge, and here there is no succession to anything except possession. Nor does the idea of succession on contract seem to be at home in Scaevola's normal usage, since almost without exception he uses *succedere* and related words to refer to universal succession[174]. Even in this text in the very next

---

[168] Cf. *Beseler*, SZ 44 (1924) 360: 'Seltsam.' and SZ 45 (1925) 454: 'Unsinn.' Contrast *C. Longo*, BIDR 14 (1901) 232.

[169] Iav. D50.17.202 lib 11 epistularum.

[170] For more detail on language, chapter III.2.(f).

[171] *A. M. Honoré*, Satura Feenstra (Fribourg, 1985) 244n29 on *et generaliter definimus*. The difference is that all his examples do go on to define something, whereas here a definition is said not to be possible.

[172] Inst. 4.15.4a.

[173] *Kaser*, RP II 286n16 with the sources.

[174] In Scaevola *succedere* occurs 13 times, *successio* 6 times and *successor* 4 times. The only

sentence the reference to *successores* is clearly in the context of universal succession[175]. The text is in fact much improved by excising the words *sive ex contractu sive voluntate*[176]. This done, there is no strange discontinuity between the two clauses, and no mention of the suspect concept of succession on contract.

§2 grants *accessio* of the seller's time to the buyer. This is one of the edictal cases so there is no problem here. But *itaque,* suggesting this as a consequence of what precedes, is odd even if §1 is thought not to be interpolated. The oddity may be due to abbreviation.

§3 is more complicated. A pledges something to his creditor B, and B then pledges it to his own creditor C[177]. The text tells us that C can add A's period of possession to his own both when the interdict is against A and when it is against a further party (D), provided that A has not repaid B.

It goes on to state that, if A has repaid B, C cannot use A's time. The distinction between the cases of A and D is dropped without warning. This must be an error, for although it is no doubt reasonable to deny C *accessio* of A's time when interdictal proceedings are between A and C and A has already repaid B, this does not seem so if C is acting against D.

But the difficulties go deeper: is it reasonable to grant C *accessio* of A's time at all? The idea of *accessio* involved here is strange. A pledge creditor had interdictal possession[178], i.e. a good claim to possession against his debtor. Yet the text has the idea of justifying his possession against the debtor not on contractual grounds granting it but by stating that the creditor has possessed for longer. This is nonsense, for if the creditor can add on to the period of his own possession the period for which his debtor has possessed, clearly the creditor can always be said to have the better claim. The reference to *accessio* where proceedings are between A and C must then be struck out; but the same does not apply to proceedings between C and D.

The reasoning in the text is *nam qui me potior est, cum ego te superaturus sim, multo magis adversus te optinere debet.* This sort of language is commonplace in

---

cases which are not unambiguously concerned with succession *mortis causa* are (a) D8.5.20.1, where it is unclear whether the successors to title mentioned are successors on sale or *mortis causa*; (b) D33.1.20.1, where a *fideicommissum* has been left of an annual payment to a priest and temple servants, and the question arises whether it is due only to those alive at the time of the bequest or also to the successors in their roles.

[175] Although exception has been taken also to this: *H. Lange,* SZ 72 (1955) 236n117, who notes it as an example of the extension to all types of succession of what originally applied only to one. Contra, *P. Lotmar,* SZ 31 (1910) 117n5, arguing that *ceteri successores* and similar expressions cannot in many cases be shown to be interpolated.

[176] *Longo,* BIDR 14 (1901) 233-4; *Beseler,* SZ 44 (1924) 360 comments only that *voluntate* is 'unverständlich'.

[177] No comment is made on the subpledge. But other examples are attested: *Kaser,* RP I 465n30; *Buckland,* Textbook 478.

[178] *Kaser,* RP I 387-9.

the context of hypothecary succession[179], where a hierarchy must be established among the various creditors and their entitlements. But it is completely out of place in the context of *accessio*. It too depends on the absurd assumption that C has the best claim because he can add three possessions (A+B+C), B is next best with two (A+B), but A has only his own period of possession. The argument ought to be rather that the pledge creditor, because of the contract, has *ipso iure* a better claim to possession than the debtor.

The conclusion seems inescapable that there are two discordant notes here. What is most likely is that the original text referred only to interdictal proceedings between C and D, and to C's entitlement to reckon towards the period of his own possession that of A and B[180]. To this an unwary hand has added the reference to proceedings between A and C, and the tempting but inapposite reasoning from *nam* to *debet*. Furthermore, the reference to repayment seems inappropriate in this context since for the interdict it is necessary only that there should be a contractual bridge in possession between A and B, and between B and C.

§4 allows *accessio* of the principal's period of possession to a buyer from a *negotiorum gestor*, provided the principal has ratified the sale. We are told that the principal was away: this may be sufficient reason for the *negotiorum gestor* to have sold the slave. The qualification about ratification seems justifiable, since otherwise the connexion between principal and buyer is rather faint; and if the principal chooses not to ratify, he will be able to vindicate the slave[181].

§5 allows the buyer of a pledge, which has been sold by a creditor on failure of repayment by his debtor, accession of the debtor's period of possession. This paragraph has caused the most interest in the literature, since it makes the legitimacy of the sale dependent on an agreement that the creditor may sell if the debtor fails to repay. It shows therefore that an express *pactum de distrahendo* was still required at Scaevola's time[182]. In spite of some scholarly opposition to this, there are texts in plenty in support of it[183]; so even though it is clear that there are some doubtful elements in Pal.192, to dispose of the proposition that an express agreement was required in order for the creditor to sell the pledge a good many more texts would have to be overturned.

---

[179] See *Heumann-Seckel* s.v. *potior*.

[180] Cf. the reconstruction of *Beseler*, SZ 44 (1924) 360.

[181] If he does ratify, he will have the *actio negotiorum gestorum* against the seller instead: C3.32.3 (AD 222) with *H.H. Seiler*, Der Tatbestand der *negotiorum gestio* im römischen Recht (Köln-Graz, 1968) 67-8.

[182] *A. Pernice* SZ 9 (1888) 208n8; *Herzen*, SZ 25 (1904) 456; *G. Schlichting*, Die Verfügungsbeschränkung des Verpfänders im klassischen römischen Recht (Karlsruhe, 1973) 2n4.

[183] Opposition from *Beseler*, Beiträge I 83 who excises *et convenerit-vendere*. But against this, see G2.64; Pomp. D13.7.8.3 lib 35 ad Sabinum; Scaev. D31.89.4 lib 4 responsorum; Scaev. D46.1.63 lib 6 responsorum; Iav. D47.2.74 lib 15 ex Cassio.

Finally, it is worth noting only that the language of *accessio* in this text is rather odd, a point which will no doubt have struck the reader of my literal translation. In the sources the standard expression appears to be *accessio temporis*[184], and the most precise is found in Ulpian: *accessio temporis marito ex persona mulieris*[185]. Qualification of the term *accessio* with a person is uncommon, although the expressions *a. auctoris* and *a. venditoris* are found in Ulpian once each[186]. They are the only parallels to *a. testatoris* in § 1[187]. Similarly *a. tui temporis* is found only here in §§ 3 and 5 and in one text of Africanus, while *a. tua* in §§ 2 and 3 is unparalleled[188]. From this in itself we cannot conclude much. But a tendency towards odd or slack expression begins to look like a feature of the LSQPT[189].

To summarise. Exception can be taken to the tentative vagueness of the *principium*, which seems neither accurate nor characteristic of classical or Justinian's law. In § 1 the words *sive ex contractu sive voluntate* interrupt the flow of the text by introducing a new and unfortunate idea. The case in § 3 is similar, where an extra point and a few words of reasoning are added. On closer inspection both turn out to be faulty. But the text appears to be substantially sound. Where additions have been made, they have the character of expansions or explanations of other points in the text. But they are well-integrated, so it appears that the whole text may have been recast to accommodate them.

11. Pal.193: D46.3.93[190]

Si duo rei sint stipulandi et alter alterum heredem scripsit, videndum an confundatur obligatio. placet non confundi. quo bonum est hoc dicere? quod, si intendat dari sibi oportere vel ideo dari oportet ipsi quod heres exstitit vel ideo quod proprio nomine ei

---

[184] VIR I.78 s.v. *accessio* II.B.

[185] D23.3.7.3 lib 31 ad Sabinum, but the phrase *ex persona* occurs only in Ulpian: D41.2.13.2, 7 and 11.

[186] D44.4.4.27 and D41.2.13.2.

[187] Or has *temporis* fallen out? E. Huschke, SZ 9 (1888) 363.

[188] Afr. D44.3.6.1; for *a. tua* cf. perhaps Paul D44.3.16 (*a. sine nostro tempore*).

[189] Cf. the terminology of *confusio* discussed under Pal.193.

[190] Translation (as emended): If there are two co-creditors and one has instituted the other heir, the question arises whether the obligation is extinguished by *confusio*. It is accepted that it is not. Why is this the correct view? Because if he makes a claim for something to be given to him, it ought to be given either because he has become heir or because it was owed to him on his own account. But there is a great difference here: for, if one of the creditors could be opposed by a temporary defence that a pact had been made, it will matter whether the heir sues on his own or on the hereditary account, so you may see whether the defence is available or not. (1) Similarly if there are two co-debtors and one has instituted the other heir, the obligation is not extinguished by *confusio*. (2) But if a principal debtor institutes his *fideiussor* heir, the obligation is extinguished by *confusio*. And something more or less general must be maintained, that where the principal obligation accedes to an accessory one, the obligation is extinguished by *confusio*; but whenever there are two principal obligations, one is added to the other to produce an action rather than *confusio*. (3) But what if the *fideiussor* has instituted the debtor heir? According to Sabinus, the obligation will be extinguished by *confusio*, although Proculus disagrees.

deberetur. atquin magna est huius rei differentia: nam si alter ex reis pacti conventi temporali exceptione summoveri poterit, intererit is qui heres exstitit utrumne suo nomine an hereditario experiatur ut ita possis animadvertere exceptioni locus sit nec ne. (1) Item si duo rei sint promittendi et alter alterum heredem scripsit, <non> confunditur obligatio. (2) Sed [et] si reus heredem fideiussorem scripserit, confunditur obligatio. et quasi generale quid retinendum est, ut ubi ei obligationi quae sequellae locum optinet principalis accedit, confusa sit obligatio: quotiens duae sint principales, altera alteri potius adicitur ad actionem quam confusionem parere. (3) Quid ergo si fideiussor reum heredem scripserit? confundetur obligatio secundum Sabini sententiam licet Proculus dissentiat.

I

This text deals with several variations on a theme: what is the effect of the coincidence in one person of two obligations for the same thing? Four cases are discussed: succession of one correal creditor to another; of one correal debtor to another; of *fideiussor* to principal; and of principal to *fideiussor*. The four cases fall naturally into two groups, dealing with the confluence of two principal obligations and that of a principal and an accessory.

The text presents few dogmatic difficulties; the same issues are discussed elsewhere in the Digest and the same solutions propounded[191].

Ven. D45.2.13 lib 3 stipulationum[192]. Si reus promittendi altero reo heres extiterit, duas obligationes eum sustinere dicendum est. nam ubi quidem altera* differentia obligationum esse possit, ut in fideiussore et reo principali, constitit alteram ab altera perimi: cum vero eiusdem duae potestatis sint non potest repperiri qua altera potius quam alteram consummari. ideoque et si reus stipulandi** heres exstiterit duas species obligationis eum sustinere.

*altera] aliqua *edd.* **reo stipulandi *ins. Mo.*

---

[191] It is for this reason that the emendations in §§ 1 and 2 can be accepted, since otherwise the text of Scaevola not only contradicts the others but is inconsistent with itself.

[192] Translations: (Venuleius) If a debtor has become heir to his co-debtor, it must be said that he bears two obligations. For when there can be some difference between the obligations, as in the case of surety and principal, it is agreed that one is consumed by the other; but when the two are of the same force, no reason can be found why one rather than the other should be extinguished. And so too if a creditor becomes heir to his co-creditor he has two obligations.

(Ulpian) Julian says that generally someone who has become heir to a person for whom he had stood surety is freed from the accessory obligation and is liable only as heir of the debtor. Then he wrote that, if a *fideiussor* has become heir to the man for whom he entered the *fideiussio,* he is liable as debtor but freed of the *fideiussio.* But when a debtor succeeds his co-debtor he is obliged on two grounds. For it cannot be seen which obligation should extinguish which; but this can be seen in the case of surety and principal because the obligation of the principal is fuller. For when there is some difference between the obligations it can be established that one extinguishes the other; but when two are of the same force no reason can be found why one rather than the other should be consumed. He relates these to the case in which he wants to show that it is not new that two obligations should coincide in one person. This happens in such a case: if a debtor has become heir to his co-debtor he bears two types of obligation; similarly if a creditor has become heir to his co-creditor he will have two types of obligation. Clearly if he should have sued on one obligation he will consume both, precisely

Ulp. D46.1.5. lib 46 ad Sabinum. Generaliter Iulianus ait eum qui heres exstitit ei pro quo intervenerat liberari ex causa accessionis et solummodo quasi heredem rei teneri. denique scripsit, si fideiussor heres extiterit ei pro quo fideiussit, quasi reum esse obligatum, ex causa fideiussionis liberari: reum vero reo succedentem ex duabus causis esse obligatum. nec enim potest repperiri quae obligatio quam peremat: at in fideiussore et reo repperitur quia rei obligatio plenior est. nam ubi aliqua differentia est obligationum, potest constitui alteram per alteram peremi: cum vero duae eiusdem sint potestatis non potest repperiri cur altera potius quam altera consumeretur. refert autem haec ad speciem in qua vult ostendere non esse novum ut duae obligationes in unius persona concurrant. est autem species talis. si reus promittendi reo promittendi heres extiterit duas obligationes sustinet: item si reus stipulandi exstiterit heres rei stipulandi duas species obligationis sustinebit. plane si ex altera earum egerit utramque consumet, videlicet quia natura obligationum duarum quas haberet ea esset, ut cum altera earum in iudicium deduceretur altera consumeretur.

The linguistic resemblances between these two texts are striking; it is enough to refer to their use of *repperiri* and *peremi, ubi aliqua differentia, eiusdem potestatis* and *duas species obligationis sustinere*. Such similarities suggest a common source. That is not far to seek, since Ulpian is citing Julian. It is possible that Venuleius cited him without acknowledgement, but just as reasonable (and more flattering to Venuleius) to suppose that the compilers struck out the attribution.

The rationale of the decision is plainly stated by Ulpian and Venuleius: if it cannot be determined which obligation should consume the other then both remain. Scaevola's approach is rather different. *Quo bonum est hoc dicere*[193]? The question demands not the reasons themselves but why they are good reasons.

In the third and fourth variants *confusio* is said to occur, whether it is the accessory that succeeds the principal[194] or the other way round[195]. Proculus however treated the cases differently and denied that *confusio* took place if the principal succeeded the *fideiussor*. The other texts are silent on this dissent; Scaevola too is silent on its motivation[196].

because it is the nature of the two obligations which he has that when one of them is brought to court both are consumed.

[193] It is an unusual expression, which occurs only in direct questions in Ulp. D37.4.3.11 lib 39 ad edictum; Ulp. D37.4.10.4 (itp) lib 40 ad edictum; Gai. D16.1.13.2 lib 9 ad edictum provinciale; and in an indirect question in Ulp. D7.1.13.2 lib 18 ad Sabinum.

[194] Pap. D46.1.50 lib 37 quaestionum; Pap. D46.3.95.3 lib 28 quaestionum; Ulp. D46.1.5 lib 46 ad Sabinum.

[195] Jul. D46.1.14 lib 47 dig; Afr. D46.1.21.2 lib 7 quaestionum; Pap. D42.6.3pr lib 27 quaestionum.

[196] The controversy is no.39 in *D. Liebs*, ANRW II.15 (1976) 259. There has been some disagreement as to whether there was a real school controversy: G. Baviera, Le due scuole dei giureconsulti romani (Florence, 1898) 119; *Krueger*, Geschichte 161n8 (162). The argument of P. Kretschmar, Die Theorie der Confusion (Leipzig, 1899) 25-28 that the Proculians had a purely practical reason for departing from the principle of *confusio*, namely that the accessory obligation could often on account of the solvency of the accessory but insolvency of the principal be the more valuable, seems plausible. The Sabinians maintained principle but were perhaps compelled to adopt the somewhat anomalous solution proposed in Pap. D42.6.3pr, allowing the *beneficium separationis* in spite of the fact that the accessory obligation was regarded as extinguished.

For the understanding of the LSQPT as a whole it is not these dogmatic points but the study of the language and argumentation of the text that is most important. The text presents two main arguments, in the *principium* and in §2; §§1 and 3 are mere statements of fact.

II

This is the argument of the *principium*. The point of denying that *confusio* takes place when one principal creditor succeeds another is this: the creditor must sue either on his own claim or on the one he has inherited. But if an *exceptio* alleging a pact not to sue could have blocked one of the claims then it will make a difference which claim is brought, so that you can see whether the *exceptio* is applicable.

This conclusion is rather dismal. It could surely have been seen whether the *exceptio* was relevant in any case; and the surviving creditor would surely know whether he had himself entered a *pactum de non petendo*. The matter however is more serious than this. The argument is not simply irrelevant but incorrect. For the *intentio* of the *actio certae creditae pecuniae* did not state the ground for the claim. Which claim the surviving creditor was bringing would not necessarily be clear unless there was a *praescriptio* in the formula. And the defendant could obtain an *exceptio pacti* automatically, the burden of proving it lying on him. So in either case the *exceptio* might well feature in the formula. The *exceptio pacti* on the other hand did state between which persons a pact had been made. Its wording was *si inter Am Am et Nm Nm non convenit ne ea pecunia peteretur*[197]. In the formula therefore it was at once clear against which claim the defendant was alleging that he had the defence of a pact: what more simple than for the plaintiff to plead on the basis of the other claim?

The text of Scaevola is troubled about a matter which for the plaintiff is not a problem. The text assumes that the ground for the claim must be clear in the formula; that the defendant will on that basis decide whether to apply to have an *exceptio* added; and that the plaintiff may be in real danger of losing his claim owing to the *exceptio*. All these assumptions are inaccurate. Its author misunderstands the operation of the formulary system.

The other texts are not much concerned with the reason why *confusio* does not take place, and state simply that it is not clear which obligation would survive. If a reason for one obligation to dispose of the other cannot be found then nothing happens. This suggests that it is not the cases in which *confusio* does not occur which need to be explained, but those in which it does. For example, if a creditor succeeds his debtor it is plain that the obligation lapses, since there is a

---

[197] *Lenel*, EP 501; G4.119.

conceptual difficulty in having both parties to it contained in one person[198]. Similarly if a debtor succeeds his surety; there is conceptual difficulty in dealing with a person who is his own surety[199]. But no such problem afflicts the case of creditor succeeding creditor.

These general points coupled with the lame procedural reasoning[200] in Scaevola's text throw some doubt on the genuineness of the whole argument from *quo bonum est hoc dicere* to the end of the *principium*. On the one hand it uses the language of the classical formulary procedure with precision (*intendat dari sibi oportere*) but on the other the conclusions drawn from the procedural argument suggest a lack of familiarity with actual practice. Accurate in form, the words are empty of substance. It is hard to suppose that they are Scaevolan, and if they are not Scaevolan, they represent a most interesting type of addition to his text: academic (since familiar with the language but not with the practice) and classicising (since referring to a form of procedure now obsolete).

III

To turn to the argument in §2. The main legal point it raises is unproblematic, since attested elsewhere, but it is objectionable in form and vague in content. 'It is a more or less general rule that when a principal obligation accedes to an accessory one there is *confusio*; where two principal obligations come together there is no *confusio* but instead one is added to the other to give an action.' This is poor Latin: the grammar fails at or around *potius... quam*, but there are oddities even before, notably *quasi generale quid* ('a sort of general something') which is so uninformative as to be pointless. Some meaning might be imported if we were to read the more normal *hoc* instead of *quid*.

The reasoning here is unsatisfactory. Where it is a matter of the confluence in one person of two actions or of two debts (rather than of one claim which offsets one debt) there is no question of there not being an action. To be told therefore that when two principal obligations come together there is an *actio* rather than *confusio* is to be told nothing, for there would be an action even if there were *confusio*. The question is rather whether in such a situation there are two actions, separately actionable.

It remains to say a few words on the terminology of this text in relation to others. The two other texts in which the same problems are discussed have

---

[198] Pomp. D46.3.107 lib 2 enchiridii; Pap. D46.1.50.

[199] Afr. D46.1.21.2 ad fin.

[200] For more lame procedural reasoning see Ulp. D46.1.5, where at the end the point is correctly made that the bringing of one of the actions will consume both, but the argument then appended that if the claimant brings one action he will consume both because the nature of the actions is such that if he brings one he will consume both.

already been cited. That they are closely parallel was also noted. The comparison with Scaevola is instructive. Venuleius and Ulpian/Julian use concrete terms. If two principal obligations come together then the creditor or debtor is said *duas obligationes sustinere*. In contrast Scaevola refers only to the occurrence or not of *confusio*. The other texts speak of one obligation 'consuming' the other, and so make it plain that only one obligation remains intact, as well as indicating which one that is. But Scaevola adheres to the more abstract and less clear *confunditur obligatio*[201].

The divergence of Scaevola's terminology is hard to explain. In other texts a clear link has been found between Scaevola and Julian. That is by no means evident here, since the terms presumably employed by Julian are not used. Yet some links can be made between Scaevola and the texts of Ulpian and of Venuleius: in both there is the use of *differentia*, but in a different context; in the former there is the use of *generaliter* where Scaevola uses *generale*; in both there is *potius quam*, accompanied in the text of Venuleius by the same sort of disturbance of the grammar as is found in the text of Scaevola. Coincidence?

Dogmatically in order, this text nonetheless displays two pieces of unsatisfactory argumentation. Both seem intelligent enough at first sight, but on inspection appear somewhat flawed. Their grasp of classical law is not so faint, however, as to suggest that we should place them very remote from the classical period.

12. Pal.194: D46.7.21[202]

Si unus ex fideiussoribus ob rem non defensam conventus sit, deinde postea res defendatur, alter fideiussorum ob rem iudicatam conveniri potest. et si reus promittendi duobus heredibus relictis decesserit, alter rem non defendat alter defendat: is qui non defendat ob rem non defensam conveniri potest, ille qui defendat ob rem iudicatam, quoniam in unius eiusdemque persona non posse committi has duas clausulas creditur et nos dicimus semper praevalere rei iudicatae clausulam eamque solam committi.

---

[201] *Confunditur obligatio:* the expression is found in six other texts according to VIR. In the following four, *confusio* results when creditor succeeds debtor (or *vice versa*). It is thus correct to say *confunditur obligatio* since there is only one obligation, the original two parties to which are now one: Pap. D46.3.95.2; Paul D46.1.71pr lib 4 quaestionum; Paul D36.1.61pr lib 4 quaestionum; Claudius apud Scaev. D36.1.82 lib 5 digestorum. In Afr. D46.1.21.4 although an accessory obligation is involved the text is specific: *confusa prima obligatione posteriorem duraturam [respondit]*. In Ulp D49.14.29.2 lib 8 disputationum the statement is general: *obligationes quas adeundo confudit non restituuntur*. The result of this examination is to show that the expression *confunditur obligatio* is used on all other appearances precisely or at least unambiguously.

There is little reason however to think the less precise use of the expression post-classical, since the post-classical sources show great consistency in using the term *confusio* (or verb *confundere*) to apply to *collatio bonorum*: PS 5.9.4 with IP 5.10.4; IT 4.2.1 and 5.1.5 (both on laws of AD396). The only exception appears to be a law of AD213 cited in the Appendix legis Romanae Visigothorum I.3 (in FIRA II 670) *actio... adita hereditate confusa est*. This is a case of succession by a creditor to his debtor, so falls into the category of precise usage.

I

If one *fideiussor* has been sued for failure to defend, and a subsequent defence has been made, then the other *fideiussor* can be sued for the judgement debt[203]. Similarly if the debtor under a stipulation dies leaving two heirs, and one defends while the other does not, the heir who failed to defend can be sued for failure to defend, the heir who defended for the judgement debt. The remainder of the fragment contains the reasoning for the decisions outlined and will be considered later.

The text is concerned with the *cautio iudicatum solvi*[204], the processual guarantee which had to be given by the defendant in the following circumstances[205]: (1) in an *actio in rem* (when process was *per formulam petitoriam*); (2) in an *actio in personam* (a) when defended by a *procurator*, and in two special cases (b) if the defendant was suspect or bankrupt, and (c) if the action was the *actio iudicati, depensi,* or *de moribus mulierum*. The rationale of the *cautio* is plain. Since there was no obligation to defend an *actio in rem*, it was only through the *cautio* that the defendant became obliged to defend; where there was representation through a *procurator* in an *actio in personam*, it was only through the *cautio* that the principal became obliged to pay the judgement debt.

The *cautio* was a *satisdatio*; its main advantage lay in the fact that is provided securities[206]. The principal or *procurator* gave the promise; the securities promised *idem*. The wording appears to have been the following[207]:

---

[202] Translation: If one surety has been summoned for failure to defend, and later a defence is taken up, the other surety may be sued for the judgement debt. And if a debtor has died leaving two heirs, one may fail to defend while the other defends; the first can be summoned for failure to defend, the second for the judgement debt, since it is thought that these two clauses cannot become actionable in respect of one and the same person, and we say that the clause on the judgement debt always takes precedence and that it alone becomes actionable.

[203] *Lenel*, Pal. ad loc. proposes that Scaevola wrote of *sponsores* not *fideiussores*. Of course there are differences (heritability; extent of liability etc; cf. note 210) but none of these features in the present text, so the amendment is not justified.

[204] *Lenel*, EP 530- thinks the text was concerned originally with the *cautio pro praede litis et vindiciarum* which had to be given in the case of an *actio in rem per sponsionem* (G4.91). It is not clear that this is the case in the present text (for doubts about this thesis for others, see F. La Rosa, 'La struttura della *cautio iudicatum solvi*' Labeo 2 [1956] 160-186 at 180-). The major difference between the two *cautiones* was in the phrasing regarding the amount payable: in the *cautio p.p.l.v.* the promise could not be for the judgement debt alone, as that was only the amount of the *sponsio*. Yet so far as defending the action goes (and that is the problem in this text), it is hard to see why the two should have differed: the question can therefore be left aside here.

[205] G4.91-, 101-.

[206] Since the action resulted anyway in a judgement debt, the main advantage of the *cautio* was precisely in the provision of securities: Ulp. D46.2.8.3 lib 46 ad Sabinum.

[207] I adopt the reconstruction of *La Rosa* (above, note 204) which differs in some respects from *Lenel's*. A translation: 'Do you promise that the amount judged in the issue in which I am about to act against you will be paid to me or my heir by you or your heir, and that the issue will

quod ob eam rem de qua ego tecum acturus sum iudicatum erit mihi heredive meo a te heredeve tuo solvi, eamque rem boni viri arbitratu defendi quod si ita factum non erit quanti ea res erit, tantam pecuniam dari, dolumque malum abesse afuturumque esse spondesne? (spondeo)

There are three promises. Payment of the judgement debt, proper defence, and absence of *dolus*. These three promises were also binding on the securities (since they promised *idem*)[208]; they too must therefore be prepared to take up defence of the action, that is to appear *in iure*[209]. So much by way of preliminary.

II

To turn to the first case in the text: one *fideiussor* is sued *ob rem non defensam*. For this to be possible the clause *ob rem non defensam* in the *cautio* must have become actionable. This means that no defence at all was made *in iure*, and therefore that the principal and the other *fideiussor* could also have been sued on the same ground. Since we are dealing with the post-Hadrianic period we can take it that the *fideiussor* had the *beneficium divisionis* and that although liable *in solidum* he could, if able to demonstrate the solvency of the other security, require that the action against him be restricted to his proportional share of the total[210].

A defence is later taken up. What consequences would this have for the security now being sued for failure to defend? The issue is mentioned twice by Julian: if *litis contestatio* in the suit for non-defence has passed but the judgement has not yet been made, then the security should be absolved; but if judgement and payment have been made, then there is no reclaim[211]. In the text of Scaevola it is stated that the security had been *conventus*. In the strict sense this means that *litis contestatio* but not the judgement has already taken place. If Scaevola followed the view of Julian he would therefore have to recommend absolution.

The question then arises whether the sued-but-now-absolved security still remained in any way liable under the *cautio*. If he had been sued for his whole share, then his liability must be at an end. But if he had been sued only for a part of it, a liability might remain. This all depends on the structure and interpretation

---

be defended in the estimation of an honest man, and if this is not done the amount at issue will be paid, and that no fraud is or will be involved?" "I promise".

[208] When the *cautio* had to be given is unclear; at any rate before *litis contestatio*, after which there was in any case even in an *actio in rem* an obligation between the parties.

[209] This they could do only as procurators for the principal, which seems to compel the conclusion that they must themselves give the *cautio* and offer securities.

[210] If *Lenel's* view that the text dealt with *sponsores* is adopted, then this question is simplified: while *fideiussores* had to wait for Hadrian to introduce the *beneficium divisionis*, *sponsores* were from the time of the *lex Furia* (c. 250-200 BC) automatically liable only for a proportional share.

[211] Jul. D46.7.4 and D46.7.14 lib 55 digestorum.

of the *cautio,* which is considered immediately below. It is worth noting that the explicit statement that it is the other (*alter*) who can be sued *ob rem iudicatam* suggests that the liability of the first has come to an end.

The next stage is that the second security can be sued on account of the judgement debt. Clearly then the action against the first security did not consume the whole of the claim; presumably it was in some way limited by the statement of *certa pecunia* or by a *praescriptio.* Yet after Hadrian's introduction of the *beneficium divisionis* it is plain that the first *fideiussor* cannot have been sued for the whole, unless the second was insolvent (which is not the case here, since it was apparently worth bringing a claim against him). Hence the statement that the second *fideiussor* is still liable is a commonplace.

But the matter is complicated by uncertainty surrounding the structure of the *cautio* and its interpretation[212]. First, is the *cautio* one promise applicable in three sets of circumstances? Or three promises? Views differ: while Ulpian appears to regard it as one promise, in another text he reports Marcellus in a manner in which the clauses of the *cautio* seem to be treated as independent promises[213]. Second, if the *cautio* is one promise then what is the relation between its three clauses? Several texts touch on this point, which appears to have been controversial. Those texts deal only with the relations between the clauses *ob rem non defensam* and *ob rem iudicatam,* and since that is also the issue in this text of Scaevola, the third (*dolus*) clause will be left aside in this discussion.

Ulp. D46.7.5.2 lib 77 ad edictum[214]. In hac stipulatione quia plures causae sunt una quantitate conclusae, si committeretur *statim stipulatio ex uno casu, amplius ex alio committi non potest.

*statim] semel *Krueger*

---

[212] J. Duquesne, 'La contexture générale de la *cautio iudicatum solvi*' Mél. Fitting I (1907) 321-353 at 339 and 353 reconstructs the *cautio* with a disjunction between the clause on non-defence and that on the judgement debt. This seems to me unlikely to be correct, since it would rule out the uncertainty which evidently prevailed on how to construe the *cautio* (see below). For further arguments against his reconstruction, *Lenel, EP* 534-.

[213] Ulp. D46.7.6 lib 78 ad edictum: *iudicatum solvi stipulatio tres clausulas in unum collatas habet.* Cf. Ulp. D46.4.20 lib 77 ad edictum. The difference is surely not to be explained simply by supposing that the texts are concerned with different *cautiones* (see note 204).

[214] Translations: (5.2) In this stipulation since several circumstances are connected to one amount, if the stipulation once becomes actionable in one case, it cannot become actionable further in another.

(13pr) It was asked, when the stipulation *iudicatum solvi* had been taken, whether, if someone failed to defend the issue and had later been judged in his absence, the clause for payment of the judgement debt was actionable: I said one clause in the stipulation *iudicatum solvi* contained both provision for failure to defend and for the judgement debt to be paid. Since the stipulation *iudicatum solvi* is contained in one clause, whether the issue reaches judgement or is not defended, it is rightly asked whether when it becomes actionable on one ground it may become actionable on the other. For example, if someone stipulates 'if the ship has come from Asia or Titius has become consul' it is agreed, whether the ship comes first or Titius becomes consul before that, that the stipulation is actionable. But when it has become actionable on the first ground it cannot become actionable on the other even if the condition is satisfied: for it is one

Ulp. D46.7.13pr lib 7 disputationum. Cum quaerebatur, si interposita iudicatum solvi stipulatione cum quis rem non defenderet postea ex eremodicio sententiam esset passus, an ob rem iudicatam clausula committatur: dicebam unam clausulam in stipulatione iudicatum solvi et ob rem non defensam et ob rem iudicatam in se habere: cum igitur iudicatum solvi stipulatio una cludatur clausula sive res iudicetur sive res non defendatur, merito quaeritur si <ex> altera causa committatur an ex altera rursum committi possit. ecce enim si quis stipuletur 'si navis ex Asia venerit aut si Titius consul +fuerit' constat sive navis prior venerit sive Titius consul ante factus sit committi stipulationem: sed ubi commissa est ex priore causa, ex altera licet existat condicio amplius non committitur: altera causa enim non utraque inerat stipulationi. proinde videndum stipulatio ob rem non defensam utrum commissa est re non defensa an non prius creditur commissa nisi ex stipulatione lis fuerit contestata? quod magis est: et ideo nec fideiussoribus videtur statim dies cedere ubi res coeperat non defendi. proinde si forte lis finita fuerit ad quam defensio erat necessaria vel solutione vel transactione vel acceptilatione vel quo alio modo consequenter placuit evanescere ob rem non defensam clausulam.

+fuerit] factus erit *Mo.*

The choice of example in the second text is interesting[215]. The question arises whether the two clauses are to be treated as an inclusive or exclusive disjunction. In an inclusive disjunction either X or Y or both may be true; that is, the truth of one proposition does not exclude the other. But in an exclusive disjunction, if one of X and Y is true then the other is thereby excluded. The distinction between these two forms is easily obscured by the word 'or'[216].

What of the present case? If we take *si navis ... factus erit* as an inclusive disjunction then effectively we allow two claims, one if the ship arrives, one if Titius becomes consul. If both conditions materialise then there is a free choice on which condition to ground a claim. Yet the claim is fully grounded even if only one condition materialises, and in this sense it can be said that with the satisfaction of the second condition the *stipulatio amplius non committitur*. Yet if the words are taken as an exclusive disjunction, then there is only ever one claim; if the second condition were satisfied it would not ground a further claim. It is simply ignored, and in this sense it can be said that the *stipulatio amplius non committitur.*

---

ground or the other not both that is in the stipulation. So it is a question whether the stipulation for failing to defend becomes actionable when the issue is not defended or is not thought to be actionable until *litis contestatio* on the stipulation has taken place. This is the better view: and so, when the issue has begun to be undefended, liability does not immediately arise for the sureties either. So if by chance the issue for which the defence was necessary has come to an end by payment or settlement or discharge or any other way it is consequently accepted that the clause on failure to defend becomes immaterial.

[215] The example goes back to Afr. D45.1.63 lib 6 quaestionum, where the principle that the *stipulatio amplius committi non potest* is also found. The point is therefore likely to go back to Julian. It is also worth comparing Scaev. D45.1.129 lib 12 quaestionum, a discussion of conjunctive and disjunctive conditions in which the same example is used. While the text has often been thought unclassical (see Index interpolationum), more recently *J. Miquel,* SZ 87 (1970) 101- has shown that it can be interpreted as an application of the principles of Stoic logic to a legal problem. Cf. also Cels. D31.27 lib 34 digestorum.

If there is a claim for Z on either ground X or Y, and the disjunction between X and Y is treated as exclusive, then if ground X materialises Z can be claimed on ground X, but there will never now be a claim for Z on ground Y since it is excluded by ground X. Should some obstacle arise in pursuit of the claim for Z on ground X, there will be no other claim to fall back on. Yet if X and Y are treated as an inclusive disjunction then there is no logical reason why if one's claim on ground X meets an obstacle, a claim on ground Y should not be made.

What sort of a disjunction has Ulpian in mind? Apparently an exclusive disjunction. *Aut* in the formulation is not conclusive, but the words *altera causa enim non utraque inerat stipulationi* surely are. This is in any case probable, since the system of logic that is likely to have influenced Ulpian—Stoic logic—conceived of the disjunction as exclusive[217]. This discussion is introduced by Ulpian in the context of the *cautio*. We must suppose that in his view the *cautio* was also to be interpreted as an exclusive disjunction. With the words *amplius committi non potest* Ulpian appears to mean that once the *cautio* becomes actionable on one ground it cannot become actionable on another.

While Stoic logic supported the interpretation of a disjunction as exclusive, practical grounds sometimes appealed for a different approach. Hence contention. That different views were put forward on the interpretation of dispositions in the form *ille vel ille* is made clear by a constitution of Justinian in which the rule *'aut' pro 'et' accipi* is established, a drastic legislative move putting an end to much philosophical enjoyment[218].

To return to the text. It is already clear that a claim *ob rem non defensam* can be brought only if no defence at all has been made. This means that both the debtor and the two securities mentioned by Scaevola have failed to defend, and that they must all have incurred liability for failure to defend. Yet on Ulpian's interpretation if the stipulation has become actionable *ob rem non defensam*, it cannot become further actionable: therefore all can be sued *ob rem non defensam* but nobody can be sued *ob rem iudicatam*. But a subsequent defence has been made, so it is necessary to conclude that the *fideiussor* sued *ob rem non defensam* must be absolved, and the others can no longer be sued for failure to defend since that condition no longer exists. Consequently no action on the *cautio* (if we follow Ulpian's interpretation) can be possible against anybody.

It seems likely that although the clauses *ob rem non defensam* and *ob rem iudicatam* were not explicitly framed as an excluding disjunction, it was

---

[216] Cf. *U. Klug*, Juristische Logik⁴ (Berlin-Heidelberg-New York, 1982) 26, 41.

[217] Chrysippus stressed the exclusive nature of the disjunction (*Miquel*, SZ 87 (1970) 92; *M. Frede*, Die stoische Logik [Göttingen, 1974] 93-). But the *subdisiunctivum*, with terms *quae opposita non sunt contraria* (Gellius 16.8.14) was generally familiar in the second century. It appears also in Proc. D50.16.124 lib 2 epistularum (*Miquel* 90-; *Frede* 98-).

[218] Just C6.38.4.1a (531) in which reference is made to παραδιάζευξις, precisely the Greek term for *subdisiunctivum*. In Gellius 16.8.14 the word παραδιεζευγμένον is used instead.

nonetheless possible to understand them in that way (from where else did the idea of using the example cited by Africanus and Ulpian come?). This conception of the clauses may have been encouraged by the (incorrect[219]) view that they were incompatible. In normal circumstances this view would lead to no difficulty since either a defence would be made (and a suit for the judgement debt would follow) or it would not be made (and a claim for failure to defend would be possible). Yet in the case of initial failure to defend followed by subsequent defence it is not true in practice that the satisfaction of the condition of non-defence and that of the existence of a judgement debt are mutually exclusive.

However this may be, there is good reason to think that there was a classical dispute about the interpretation of the *cautio*. It was no doubt a conflict between rigorous logic and practical suitability[220]. Scaevola appears to have been on the side of the practical, for although in his case it is plain that all (debtor and both securities) have incurred liability for not defending, nonetheless he allows an action against one security for payment of the judgement debt.

The second variant in the text is that a *reus promittendi* dies and is succeeded by two heirs, one of whom defends. That heir can be sued *ob rem iudicatam*, the heir who did not defend *ob rem non defensam*. This case raises only a few new points: (1) liability on the *cautio* is inherited, which is unproblematic[221]. (2) In contrast to the first case there is no mention of initial failure to defend. Here it sounds as if a defence was offered at once, yet the apparent difference can be attributed only to an imprecision (or abbreviation), for it is evident that without an initial failure to defend, the clause *ob rem non defensam* could not have become actionable. (3) It is natural to assume that the *reus promittendi* is the principal debtor. But this raises problems which are not discussed in the text. If the heirs are heirs of a principal debtor, then (*nomina ipso iure divisa*) there must now be two claims for two debts. But the heirs are also liable on the *cautio* (as the text makes plain) and must undertake a proper defence. The question arises whether each heir is liable only to defend for his own inherited share or also in the action against the other heir. To these points there is no reference, and only one *res* to be defended is mentioned. Consequently the most probable solution is that the *reus* is a *reus* on ground of the *cautio iudicatum solvi*. If this is so, then he is not a principal debtor but either (a) a *procurator*[222] or (b) a *fideiussor* liable on the *cautio*[223] or (c)

---

[219] A true exclusive disjunction depends on the incompatibility of the two propositions. In Ulpian this incompatibility is not forthcoming: there is no reason why the ship should not arrive and Titius be consul. But Ulpian appears to be dealing not with an incompatibility between the conditions but with one between the claims based on them. So too for the *cautio*.

[220] Ulpian in D46.7.13pr seems to suggest that the way that the logicians attempted to accommodate their views to practice was by a narrower construction of the point at which the clause *ob rem non defensam* became actionable.

[221] It might be possible to suppose that the *reus* had already at the time of his death incurred liability for failure to defend. But since the text does not state this, it is to be adopted only if necessary (and it is not).

defendant in an *actio in rem*. With the exception of these points, it is enough to refer back to the discussion of the first variant.

III

Next comes the reasoning in the text. But first a recapitulation of the conclusions of this discussion: if two securities are liable on the *cautio* and no defence is made, then both are liable *ob rem non defensam*. On Ulpian's interpretation, the incurring of a further liability *ob rem iudicatam* is thereby excluded. Scaevola however admits a claim *ob rem iudicatam* against a security who has not (yet) been sued *ob rem non defensam*.

The reasoning found at the end of this text is quite different: the two clauses cannot become actionable in relation to the same person. This comment is consistent with Ulpian's view, but is entirely inappropriate here: to admit an action *ob rem iudicatam* against the second security, as Scaevola does, is a practical measure, but he could not claim that that security was not also liable *ob rem non defensam*. Rather, he admits a claim *ob rem iudicatam* in spite of the fact that the security is already liable *ob rem non defensam*. This is therefore precisely a case in which the two clauses have become actionable in relation to the same person[224]. We can hardly suppose that the contradictory explanation was contributed by Scaevola: the words *quoniam ... creditur* are to be attributed to another hand.

The text ends with the words *et nos dicimus semper praevalere rei iudicatae clausulam eamque solam committi*. They fit badly with what precedes. In order to say that one clause prevails, we must suppose that there is a choice; in other words, that both clauses have become actionable. But this is precisely what is denied in the preceding sentence. And the conception that one can somehow choose which clause becomes actionable is strange[225]. These words therefore are inconsistent with the previous clause. That in itself is no problem, since it is unclassical. But they are also out of place in the text as a whole.

On what grounds might the clause *ob rem iudicatam* prevail? It only becomes actionable (to say nothing of prevailing) when a judgement has been given, so it is difficult to see how it can always prevail. If it is to do so, then the clause *ob rem non defensam* must be completely insignificant. And this does appear to be the

---

[222] Not a *cognitor*, for whom the main debtor gave the *cautio* (G4.101; Mod. D46.7.10 [itp] lib 4 pandectarum).

[223] Not a *sponsor* or *fideipromissor*, whose liability was not heritable (G3.120).

[224] It is worth noting that if *conveniri* had been written in place of *committi* this sentence would have been consistent with Scaevola's statements. But a confusion between the two is hardly to be attributed to Scaevola; and other texts also speak of *committi* as the relevant point.

[225] Here again it would make more sense to speak of *conveniri*.

conception of the words: in postclassical process the promise of a proper defence was superfluous, since on failure to defend even an *actio in rem* official compulsion was applied and the transfer of possession after the expiry of a set period ordered[226]. This had of course already existed in the case of an *actio in personam* but for an *actio in rem* was entirely new; the first indication of it seems to date from Diocletian[227], and at this point the clause *ob rem non defensam* became entirely superfluous. So if the one clause has become inconsequential, then it can correctly be said that the other always prevails[228]. This explanation does not flatter the postclassical intellect, but it is hard otherwise to find any sense in the sentence.

To sum up. The last two sentences cannot be attributed to Scaevola: the first contains a classical principle which is unintelligible in the context; the second is incomprehensible for classical law. But the two are incompatible with each other. What is their origin? In the case of the first sentence, little speaks for Justinian. It is striking that the text is found at all in the Digest, since the promise to defend was also superfluous under Justinian. It does not seem likely that a vague and pointless explanation for Scaevola's decision would have been added by the compilers, particularly when the legal problem could hardly have interested them. For a postclassical origin speak (1) the 'non-compilatorial' character of the interpolation; (2) *creditur*, which is odd here; (3) the application of a classical principle in an inappropriate context (possibly with a new significance). As for the second sentence, the words *nos dicimus* ... are inconsistent with what precedes, and it is perhaps more likely that they are compilatorial: (1) *nos* is appropriate for a sovereign declaration; (2) the addition of a clause at the end of a text is a compilatorial commonplace; (3) the unsympathetic dismissal of a classical problem is characteristic of Tribonian's method[229].

---

[226] *Kaser*, RZ 466.

[227] C7.43.8 (290).

[228] The penultimate sentence might be understood in this way too in a new sense: if one clause is not considered then they cannot both become actionable. This is trivial, but such a postclassical metamorphosis of the classical principle that the *stipulatio amplius committi non potest* is not impossible.

[229] Here as often it is remarkable that the compilers did not undertake a more careful revision of the text, contenting themselves instead with the addition of a sentence which in effect disposes of the entire problem in the text. Shortage of time perhaps.

III. Synthesis

1. Introduction

After analysis in the last chapter, this one turns to synthesis. In chapter II an attempt was made to separate classical and unclassical elements in the LSQPT. The unclassical elements in the work proved to be extensive, nor was it simply a matter of identifying occasional glosses or standard compilatorial interpolations, since several texts were found to contain lengthy unclassical tracts.

Around a third of the extant LSQPT cannot be classical. This is a more radical textual critical conclusion than is fashionable nowadays, but not more radical than is warranted by a close and (I hope) disciplined analysis of the remains. It is worth trying to draw some general conclusions from the individual exegeses. There seem to be two main possibilities to account for the state of the work: firstly, that it is a genuine work of Scaevola which has been subjected to extensive annotation; secondly, that it is not a work of Scaevola at all. Between these two lie several variations: for example, that it was composed from Scaevola's works but he was not the author; or that it is an epitome of one of his works.

This section considers various general aspects of the LSQPT, for example, genre, language, structure and sources, before going on to assess the three most plausible hypotheses on the work: that it is a genuine work written and published by Scaevola, but much altered; that it is spurious; that it is an epitome of the *quaestiones*. The second of these—that the work is not by Scaevola at all—may seem much more audacious than the first. But that is hardly so. For a third of the work is in any case spurious; and the remainder of it is based on classical sources. If these factors are taken as constant, then the suggestion that the author was (for instance) a teacher in a post-classical law school who put the work together from classical texts (of Scaevola?) appending his own extensive comments is not intrinsically more improbable than the theory that a similar person defaced a genuine work of Scaevola with substantial glosses. In each of the three hypotheses, we are entitled to attribute a good part of the text to Scaevola: the difference is simply that in the second and third cases the author is taken to be someone other than Scaevola, making selections in the third case from one other work attributed to Scaevola, but selecting in the second case from a wider range and perhaps also annotating more extensively; whereas in the first case we suppose that Scaevola was actually the author of a work which has then been annotated and reworked. It is up to this section to decide which hypothesis is in fact most plausible.

80   III. Synthesis

First it is necessary to recapitulate the conclusions which were reached on individual texts. The texts fall into several groups.

(1) Texts in which no significant unclassical elements were detected

186

187pr (where at most it was suggested that the compilers may have suppressed details of a classical controversy).

187.2

188pr-1

189

192.2, 4 and 5

(2) Texts subject only to minor glossing:

188.2 (*sed ... reliquis, liberis et parentibus* are glossed)

192.1 (*sive ex contractu sive voluntate* are glossed)

(3) Texts containing significant unclassical elements:

187.1 Perhaps the most striking example: the whole discussion of *causa* and *gradus*; the circular argument dependent on a non-classical premise; and some curious language indict the text. The unclassical elements involve theorising or reasoning, but in neither case of a high standard. The *causa* distinction appears to have been clumsily adapted from Julian or Ulpian.

188.3 The generalisation at the end (*quomodo ... deducitur*) seems to be interpolated, possibly inspired by Afr. D28.6.35.

190 Almost the whole of the second half of the text is incomprehensible; presumably a misunderstanding has led to this apparently senseless interpolation.

191 A difficult and very corrupt text whose original context is unclear. A good deal of it is unclassical, and two points seem to have been inspired by a reading of Julian (cited in Paul and Ulpian).

192 The *principium* or at least part of it seems to be an addition. In §3 a further case has been introduced with the insertion of the words *adversus te ipsum*; the whole sentence of reasoning has also been added. The language of *accessio* is unusual.

193 Although the dogmatic lines of the text are unobjectionable, the reasoning in pr and §2 betrays a lack of understanding of formulary procedure. The interpolation is of an academic nature; it involves the addition of historical rather than practical grounds in the reasoning. There is some odd language.

194 The facts cited conflict with the explanation given, which must be interpolated. The sentence following the explanation is also interpolated, conceivably by the compilers.

It is of course the third category which requires the most discussion. What is most striking about the unclassical material is that it is of no practical significance. It falls roughly into two groups, reasoning and generalisation. So (in Pal. 187.1, 192.3, 193pr and 2, and 194) the bulk of the postclassical element is devoted to explaining the reason for the fact or solution stated in the text. In Pal.188.3 the points made in the cases discussed are drawn out into a general rule. One might even fit the apology in Pal.192pr for the lack of a definition into this scheme. The obscurity of Pal.190 and 191 makes them harder to fit in, but the attempt to draw distinctions in Pal.191 is consistent with the broadly theoretical and academic character of the other unclassical elements.

To return to the main problem: is the work wholly spurious, or has it simply been substantially revised? Several points are relevant, but are disconcertingly inconclusive or hard to apply. (a) Do the texts fall structurally into more than one part? If this is so, then it is likely that one element is later than the other. From this it might be inferred that the work has been revised rather than composed as a whole. But that inference is not sound, since it is possible that the work is both wholly spurious and yet lacks cohesion: inconcinnities could be attributed to the failure of a postclassical author to harmonise his (classical) sources with his own remarks. (b) What are the origins of the problems? If it is possible to identify the origin of discussions in the LSQPT either in Scaevola's other works or in those of other jurists then the probability is that the work is not genuine. For it is not likely that Scaevola produced an abbreviated version of his own works, nor that he would have resorted to wholesale borrowing from other jurists. But the essence of *quaestiones* is to tackle difficult problems, often already discussed by others[1], so it is necessary to be able to distinguish between the acceptable use of the same legal material and servile imitation or plagiarism. (c) More conclusive than either of these, for what purpose and what readership might Scaevola have written the LSQPT? Into what genre of classical Roman legal writing does it fall? Or, if it is spurious, for what purpose and for what readership was it composed in post-classical times? This point too presents difficulties: although we can reach some conclusions about it on the basis of the surviving extracts of the work, we must bear in mind that these amount only to about ten per cent of the original[2], so that what survives is not necessarily a reliable guide to the original character of the work.

2. Six criteria

(a) Structure. What sort of structure do the texts containing unclassical material display? Is it plain that one element is a later addition? Or is the unclassical material well-integrated? This is a useful test which may give some

---

[1] This also accounts for the frequent citations of jurists in *quaestiones*, although in this respect the LSQPT is not characteristic: Julian is cited once, and Proculus once.

[2] The figure of roughly ten per cent is based on the work of T. Birt, Das antike Buchwesen (Berlin, 1882). Birt shows that a *liber* was of a standard length which fluctuated between 1500-2500 lines (309); and that line length similarly was standard at around 35 characters (197). Lenel's Palingenesia lines are slightly longer than this, and adjusting for that we have roughly 186 lines of the LSQPT of standard length. As a proportion of the original book this is 7.4% (on the higher figure of 2500 lines) or 12.4% (on the lower figure of 1500). Since precision is impossible, it is best to take the average of these two figures: 10%. In particular there is the difficulty of not knowing whether the lines we have or at least lines equivalent in number were written by Scaevola or, if not, at what point they were added. Any lengthy additions will distort the picture, but it is hardly possible to draw a new one.

indication of the nature of the work, but it is hard to apply objectively. Its results therefore require confirmation on other grounds.

187.1 reads like a commentary on the will quoted. Yet it is hard to view it as an interpolation, not simply on account of its scale but owing to the extent of its integration in the text. It cannot be a gloss which has moved into the text, for the words *secundum haec proposita* followed by the repetition of the clauses quoted from the will could make no sense in the margin, but have resumptive force, taking up the discussion of the will again after the reflections on *causa* and *gradus*.

190 Here the incomprehensible second half of the text seems to be an addition to the classically acceptable first half.

191 This is a hard case, since so little of the text is consistent with itself. The distinctions and general development of the argument appear to be a free composition based on a discussion of Julian (see the section on sources below).

192 The *principium* acts as an introduction to the list, and is not out of place. In §1 the gloss is easily detected. But in §3 the new point and the explanation inserted blend in well.

193 The reasoning in pr and §2 seems reasonably well integrated in the text. It is clearly unclassical, but that is for reasons of content rather than form. It could however be explained as glossing, although unusually extensive.

194 The explanation *quoniam* ... seems just to have been added at the end of the sentence.

What sort of conclusion does this material allow? Some of the texts show only additions, which are not well-integrated (Pal.190, 194). In others (Pal.187.1, 191, 192, 193) the impression given is very much that some original material has been freely re-worked. In these cases it is not a matter of glossing, but rather of paraphrasing or of free composition. Which of these is closer to the mark is hard to say; the discussion of the sources may allow a better judgement. But it is clear in several cases that elements which are evidently unclassical have been incorporated in the text to a relatively great extent. This does not necessarily show that the LSQPT was not a classical work, but only that in its extant form it has been subject to a thorough reworking.

(b) Sources. What are the sources of the LSQPT? On the hypothesis that Scaevola did publish such a work, this question needs to be answered where possible for the extraneous elements; but if we suppose that the whole is spurious, the origin of the whole must be considered. There is of course a presumption that the main source is Scaevola himself. While in the case of works identified as spurious this is more an uninspiring compromise than a necessary conclusion[3], special circumstances apply to this instance. To take a better known example: Ulpian's *opiniones* employ considerable material not obtained from his works. Why the attribution? Because Ulpian was the best known of all jurists, and his name therefore good for sales and good for citing. Contrast the case of Scaevola. The LSQPT uses much material from Julian. Why the attribution to

---

[3] Cf. *D. Liebs*, TR 41 (1973) 295-6.

2. Six criteria 83

Scaevola? If it is a wholly spurious work it would make sense to attribute it to Julian, a more famous name. The crucial differences between the case of the *opiniones* and that of the LSQPT are therefore two: Scaevola is not at the pinnacle of juristic fame; there is evidence of the use of a more charismatic source, which there can be no motive to conceal.

To be specific: Julian stands out as the major quarry for the LSQPT. Several texts show evidence of borrowing from him. This is most notable and unequivocal in the following cases:

> 187.1: the *causa/gradus* discussion is adapted from Julian in book 30 of his *digesta*, cited by Ulp. D28.6.10.7 lib 4 ad Sabinum.
>
> 191 : the reference to *gratificatio* comes from *gratificatus* in Julian cited by Paul D42.5.6.2 lib 58 ad edictum.
>
> : the reference to *vigilantia* comes from Julian cited by Ulpian in D42.8.6.7 lib 61 ad edictum.

Other cases are individually less clear, yet in a high proportion of the texts in the LSQPT there is a problem for which a parallel can be found in the work of Julian, and where referring to that text of Julian aids the understanding of the text in the LSQPT. In comparison there are few cases where the works of other jurists need be invoked. For these purposes of course I do not distinguish between Julian and Africanus[4]:

> 188pr-1: Julian D35.2.87.7 lib 61 digestorum
> 188.2-3 : Africanus D28.6.35 lib 5 quaestionum
> 193 : Julian cited in Ulpian D46.1.5 lib 46 ad Sabinum
>   cf. Africanus D46.1.21.2 lib 7 quaestionum
> 194 : Julian D46.7.4 and 14pr lib 55 digestorum
>   : cf. Africanus D45.1.63 lib 6 quaestionum

The clearest case in which a jurist other than Julian or Africanus provides the best parallel to the problem in the LSQPT is Pal.187.2, where Neratius D28.5.55 lib 1 membranarum deals with the same material.

It is difficult to determine the relationship between Julian and the LSQPT. The problem is whether the situation is (1) that a text has been borrowed in its entirety from Julian and reworked, or (2) that references to Julian have been added to a text of another origin[5].

(1) Complete borrowing: it is only in the case of Pal.191 that this can be shown convincingly. Even in Pal.187.1, while the borrowing and adaptation is extensive, it seems to be imposed on an already existing text. In particular it is not possible to show that the problematic clauses quoted from the will originated in a discussion of Julian's. And since the textual disturbances are detectable precisely

---

[4] The clearest cases are cited in the text. A few more remote ones are: on 188, Jul. D30.94pr; on 190, Jul. D36.1.28.3-4 and cf. Jul. apud Ulp. D28.6.2.2; on 191, Jul. D29.2.44.

[5] The first of these is *a priori* less probable, since an attribution to Julian would then be more likely.

because intelligible doctrines from Julian have been employed in inappropriate contexts, there is plainly another element in the texts to explain, whether this is to be attributed to a classical hand or a later writer.

Pal.193 is a less clear case. In spite of the use of different terminology, some verbal links and the use of (unsatisfactory) procedural reasoning in both texts may suggest that the Scaevolan text is a rewriting of Ulp. D46.1.5 in which Julian is cited.

(2) Adding references to Julian: the suggestion that an original text has been annotated by a 'Juliankenner' is supported by Pal.188.2-3 if it is accepted that the origin of the final generalisation is to be found in a text of Africanus.

A few texts which are parallel to rather than plainly derived from Julian remain: Pal.188pr-1 and 194. The origin cannot be shown, so it is unclear whether Scaevola may have discussed similar problems to those in Julian.

This is a curious and problematic relationship, which seems to demonstrate (a) adaptation of original material in accordance with points made by Julian and (b) a tendency to select for the LSQPT problems discussed by Julian. But how is this plain but somehow ambiguous connexion with a single source to be explained? Generally, such dependence on one source must cast doubt on the authenticity of a classical work, even though relations of dependence do exist between some classical works[6]. This in itself does not allow us to eliminate the possibility that Scaevola derived much material from Julian himself. But the link between the LSQPT and Julian in Pal.187.1 and 191 is plainly based on annotation and adaptation by a later hand, so if we suppose (as we might) that Scaevola was himself in some degree dependent on Julian, then this tendency has evidently been exacerbated by the *adnotator*.

(c) Genre. Unevenness is the hallmark of the LSQPT. This makes it difficult to assign to a genre of classical legal writing. The fragment on *accessio* (Pal.192) and that on the occurrence of *confusio* (Pal.193) would be at home in an institutional work. Others, such as the complex will (Pal.187.1), are eminently suited to be the subject of advanced discussion and therefore to be recorded in a work of *quaestiones*; and others too (for example Pal.187pr and 194) would be appropriate there, since they admit of differing interpretation.

It would be wrong to exaggerate the force of the classical jurists' conception of genre, for there are some oddities among their productions[7]. Yet it is remarkable that almost all their works fall into a few clearly defined categories: institutions, *responsa, quaestiones* (sometimes called *disputationes*), and (later) monographs.

---

[6] The most obvious is Africanus' borrowing from Julian; but Ulpian's book 4 *ad Sabinum* is also heavily dependent on Julian's book 30 *digestorum: P. de Francisci,* BIDR 22 (1910) 160n2.

[7] Notably Pomponius' *liber singularis enchiridii*. But Marcian's *institutiones* too are odd (described by *Schulz,* History 172-3 = Geschichte 208-9 as a 'literary monstrosity', though this he takes to be an argument against Marcian's having published it himself).

The purpose and the intended readership for each category are never in doubt. Classical law (as was pointed out in the introduction) did not regard the monograph as the normal form in which to publish collections of legal problems. So the LSQPT refuses to allow itself to be classified.

As for style, this is also variable. Some fragments are laconic and read in the form of *responsa* (Pal.187pr, 189). Others indulge in jurisprudential rambling (Pal.187.1, 191) which would be more suited to *quaestiones*. Some is animated (Pal.191), and some rather arid (Pal.192). The main feature which unites many of the fragments is that they are formally well-structured. Arguments are slowly and gradually expounded (even if they are faulty: Pal.187.1) and each step is listed; variations on a theme are developed (Pal.192, 193); distinctions are drawn (Pal.191). All this has a somewhat academic flavour about it.

The work seems formally suited to school use. Yet the paradox is that it does not fit into the classical schema of legal education: *instituere, audire* and *disputare, adsidere*[8]. And it does not belong to any of the recognised genres of Roman legal writing. The search for a motive for writing the work and the hunt for a readership must therefore draw a blank. This must raise suspicion that the LSQPT is not a classical work.

(d) Location. If the LSQPT was either altered or composed in postclassical times, then the place to begin the search is clearly in a postclassical law school. Where was the relevant school? The eastern law schools are on the whole better documented, especially that at Beirut, but there was a school at Rome which remained important through the fourth century and existed beyond[9]. While more is known of the East, until the fifth century it is not much more. *Collinet*, in his account of the history of the law school at Beirut[10], is forced to concede that there is complete obscurity as to its programme of teaching until c.AD410[11], and that the publications produced by its law teachers up till that time are also unknown[12]. The lacunae are regrettable, since it is precisely on these two points that the attempt to place the LSQPT depends: was it the sort of work which might have been used in teaching? is it in conformity with the known scholarly output of the school?

---

[8] On classical legal education see particularly D. *Liebs*, ANRW II.15 (1976) 197-286 with further literature.

[9] F. *Wieacker*, SZ 67 (1950) 398; J. *Gaudemet*, La formation du droit séculier et du droit de l'Église aux IVe et Ve siècles (Paris, 1957) 82. On western law schools in general: E. *Volterra*, 'Western postclassical law schools' Cambridge Law Journal 10 (1949) 196-207; 'Appunti sulle scuole postclassiche occidentali' Annali di storia del diritto 1 (1957) 51-65. More generally still, M. *Conrat*, 'Zur Kultur des röm. Rechts im Westen des röm. Reichs im vierten und fünften Jh. nach Christi' Mél. Fitting I (Montpellier, 1907) 289-320.

[10] P. *Collinet*, Histoire de l'école de droit de Beyrouth (Paris, 1925).

[11] ibid. 219-.

[12] ibid. 263-.

East or West? This is in the end a question of availability and access. If we believe that the LSQPT is genuine, then the problem is where such a (presumably) obscure work can have been available. If we prefer to believe it to be spurious, then given the undeniable influence on it of high classical sources (especially Julian's *digesta*) the problem is where those sources could have been available. It is well-known that the libraries of the Eastern law schools had access to much obscure material[13]. Julian would certainly have been available; a minor work of Scaevola probably. In the West there are few places where this is at all probable, except for Rome where even in AD370 there remained twenty eight public libraries. If we are to look for the LSQPT outside the eastern cities of Beirut, Constantinople, Alexandria and Caesarea, then it is only in Rome that we can expect to find it[14]. Since however the work or its sources may have been available both in Rome and in the library of an eastern law school, the criterion of availability is ultimately unhelpful in deciding between East and West.

Some have been impressed with linguistic arguments, which are relevant if we adopt the hypothesis of annotation. *Collinet* notes that between AD380 and 420 the school at Beirut moved from tuition in Latin to adopt tuition in Greek[15]. In spite of some evidence to the contrary, most (particularly Libanius) is in favour of the use of Latin throughout the fourth century[16]. Yet few conclusions can legitimately be drawn from discovering what the language of teaching at Beirut was at any given point[17]: the fact that from the fifth century teaching took place in Greek does not demonstrate that a work with Latin annotations either cannot have been annotated at Beirut or was annotated there before about AD420. If the Latin could be read there, then additions in that language could also have been made (even if Greek professors would normally be expected to make their notes in Greek), particularly as much can be shown to have been inspired by or adapted from other Latin texts. All this means that the linguistic argument against the origin of Latin glosses in Beirut after AD420 is too weak to be useful.

The content of the work is also unhelpful for locating it geographically. Pal.192 deals with the interdict *utrubi*. As *Levy* pointed out[18], postclassical law simplified the procedure for regulating possessory disputes by abandoning one of the interdicts. The East continued to use only the interdict *uti possidetis*, while the West employed *utrubi*. This may suggest that the LSQPT aimed for the western market. On the other hand, the Digest uses the fragment not in the

---

[13] *Gaudemet*, Formation 79.

[14] *Wieacker*, Textstufen klassischer Juristen (Göttingen, 1960) 107.

[15] *Collinet*, École 212-.

[16] Cf. *F. Pringsheim*, SZ 69 (1952) 398-402 citing P. Ryl 474; but see Libanius *or.* 62.21-23 on the flood of young men to the law school at Berytus; elsewhere he complains of law and Latin in the same breath, especially in *or.* 2.44; 48.22; for detail see *J.H.W.G. Liebeschuetz*, Antioch (Oxford, 1972) 242-.

[17] Cf. *Pringsheim*, ibid. 401.

[18] *E. Levy*, SZ 49 (1929) 239 (= Gesammelte Schriften I 169).

context of *utrubi* at all, but in relation to positive prescription. Either East or West could have employed it in that context, so this argument is therefore also inconclusive.

Some help may be gained from the character of the unclassical elements. It is a commonplace that the East is to be associated with scholia, the West with paraphrase[19]; similarly postclassical compositions from the East are generally held to have a more speculative and less practical character than those of the West[20]. Into which mould does the LSQPT fit? In the section on structure, it was remarked that the work does not seem to break down simply into text and gloss. Instead some texts have the character of a paraphrase. This would tend to point West. Yet it can hardly be said to have a practical character.

(e) Content. Most striking in view of the unevenness of form is the considerable uniformity of content of the LSQPT. Most of the fragments deal with the law of succession. Within this, the law relating to pupils and their abstention (Pal.190, 191) and to pupillary substitution (Pal.187.2, 188) is particularly prominent. It is in the context of inherited liabilities that Pal.193 can also be placed, so the only exceptions, which are not concerned with succession, are Pal.192 and 194. It is true that in both of these heirs are mentioned, but the main question in Pal.192 is *accessio* for the purposes of the interdict *utrubi,* and *accessio* on succession is not treated at any length. Similarly, while Pal.194 does consider a case of succession, that does not appear to be the main problem of the fragment.

The content is disappointing for an attempt to judge from it where and when the LSQPT may have been produced or revised. In Pal.187.1 the premise that liberty prevails seems unclassical but there is no evidence when it became general dogma. In Pal.194 the interpretation suggested for the last clause would allow us to place the text after approximately AD290. But this cannot be certain. No other elements allow any more precision.

As for the order of the fragments, the reconstruction produced by Lenel is of course arbitrary, since it follows the order of the fragments in the Digest. But a *liber singularis* gives no firm ground for reconstructing the order in which extant fragments are to be placed, so it does not seem possible to improve on this arbitrariness.

(f) Language. The consequences which may be drawn from the study of juristic language are controversial. Yet few would deny that individual jurists have individual characteristics. To name but two, *plane*[21] and *aequissimus*[22] are both

---

[19] *Kaser,* RP II 32; *Levy,* ibid. 237 (= GS I 168).

[20] *Levy,* ibid. 237, 240 (= GS I 167, 170).

[21] It occurs 301 times in Ulpian, but only 43 times in Paul.

[22] 80 out of 86 instances are in Ulpian: *Honoré,* Ulpian 79 (a point accepted by *B. W. Frier* reviewing Ulpian in Michigan Law Review 82 (1984) 859).

expressions favoured by Ulpian[23]. Similarly in the case of Scaevola it is not hard to think of characteristic turns of phrase. Of these the most obvious is *secundum ea quae proponerentur*[24], an expression which is found very frequently in his *responsa* and *digesta* where he limits the applicability of the *responsum* he is delivering to the facts outlined in the *quaestio*. A close study of Scaevola would no doubt reveal other elements peculiar to his style[25].

Such a study lies outside the scope of these remarks. The inevitable consequence is that the few points made here cannot hope to convince either that the language of the LSQPT is characteristically Scaevolan or that it is so remote from his normal usage that he cannot possibly be the author.

Yet there is in any case a great gulf between detecting a style and assessing the authenticity of a work. Style can change; and 'characteristic' elements can be assimilated by other authors. So an unfamiliar style may be characteristic of a period of creativity from which no other works of a particular author survive; and a familiar one may be the imitation of a disciple.

This does not mean that there is no value in the study of individual style. But if these difficulties are borne in mind, then ultimately our judgement whether a text is genuine or not must depend on an analysis of content as well as language. This is accepted also in the work of the scholar most committed to linguistic research, Professor *Honoré*. In some remarks on the use of linguistic indicators for the study of interpolations in the Digest[26], he establishes firstly that *refragari* is a word characteristic of Papinian (eleven out of nineteen instances in the Digest are in texts of Papinian) but secondly that three out of the eleven instances in Papinian are probably interpolated[27]. The necessary conclusion from this is that the study of juristic language can allow us to make a judgement on style, but not on the authenticity of an individual text.

Chapter II analysed the legal content of the individual texts in the LSQPT. It concluded that a good deal of what is extant cannot be attributed to Scaevola. And if it is true that linguistic evidence can be used to allow us to draw

---

[23] The first of these may well be the more significant, since minor points of usage can be largely independent of particular contexts. Cf. *A. Rodger*, Oxford Journal of Legal Studies 3 (1983) 386; *R. Syme*, SZ 97 (1980) 94.

[24] Already noted by *W. Kalb*, Roms Juristen nach ihrer Sprache dargestellt (Leipzig, 1890) 103.

[25] So far as the choice of vocabulary is concerned, an examination can easily be carried out using *T. Honoré* and *J. Menner*, Concordance to the Digest Jurists (Oxford, 1980). But other features of style are important and not so easily measured, such as word order and the length of sentences. These may provide a more accurate guide to style: see *Frier*, (op.cit., n.22) 861 with further literature.

[26] *Honoré*, 'Some suggestions for the study of interpolations' TR 49 (1981) 225-249 at 229-233. Cf. also his recent study 'Techniques of interpolation' in Sodalitas: scritti in onore di A. Guarino (Naples, 1985) 2723-2738.

[27] The interpolator may pick up elements of the style of the source he is interpolating, as *Honoré* suggests in TR 49 (1981) 238, 247.

2. Six criteria

conclusions only about style but not also about authenticity, then it is plain that even impeccable Scaevolan style will not redeem a passage which is unclassical in content. The language of the LSQPT, however, is not impeccably Scaevolan, and in spite of the preference I have expressed for analysis of content, it is an interesting exercise to see how far unclassical content is matched by uncharacteristic form.

These lists contain only a few verbal peculiarities; this for reasons of economy (of effort). Texts from the LSQPT are cited according to Lenel's Palingenesia. All other texts cited without qualification are texts of Scaevola.

I Some words not found in Scaevola outside the LSQPT[28]

atquin	Pal.193pr	definire	Pal.192pr
omnino	Pal.188pr	distinguere	Pal.191
plane	Pal.192.1	extorquere	Pal.191
quippe	Pal.187.1		
sin vero	Pal.187.2 and 191		

II Some notes on usage in Scaevola and in the LSQPT[29]

(i) *creditur* is found only in Pal.194 and in D20.4.21.1. The exegesis above argued that the use in the LSQPT, where it means 'it is believed', is inappropriate. And in the only other case, D20.4.21.1, it is (a) emended, and more importantly (b) means 'it [money] is lent'. (The other two instances cited in CDJ are notes of Tryphoninus.)

(ii) *didicimus* is found only in Pal.187.1; or also in Pal.194, if van de Water's emendation from *dicimus* (which itself is found only there and in D15.1.51) is accepted.

(iii) *differentia* is only in Pal.193 and D33.2.38pr.

(iv) *generale* and *generaliter*. The adjective is found five times, of which four are concerned with testamentary interpretation: a disposition has been made to an individual and a general disposition has also been made. The question is the effect on the individual of the general disposition. The fifth case, a different situation, is Pal.193.2.

Similarly the adverb is used three times of general provisions in a will, and a fourth time in a similar context (D28.2.29.6). The fifth appearance, Pal.192pr, is unparalleled.

(v) *in libris suis* is found in Pal.187.1. There are no other references to *libri* in Scaevola, and the singular is found only once (D13.1.18).

(vi) *manifestare, manifestus* and *manifeste.* The most common contexts for all of these are particularly (a) elucidation of a testator's intention, and (b) supplying manifest evidence. These are the contexts of eighteen out of twenty appearances (including the superlative adverb which occurs once). The exceptions are Pal.187.1 and D34.1.16.1[30]

---

[28] I list only those which seem to me in some way significant. Some others include *principaliter, adferre, immutare, intendere, vigilare, superfluus, mortalitas, optio, paganus, sequella.* This list may not be exhaustive.

[29] Again I give here only the instances which seem more significant. Others include *condicionalis, irritum, iuste, neglegere* and *neglegentia, nullo pacto, numquid, porro.*

[30] But note that *Kalb* (op.cit., n.24) 105 raises no objections to *manifestare.* For *manifeste* see Honoré, in Sodalitas 2735.

(vii) *omnimodo.* Three out of six appearances are in the LSQPT (Pal.192.4, and twice in Pal.190). The remainder are D15.1.51, D32.37.2, and D34.4.30.4.

(viii) *in perpetuum* occurs three times, twice in D33.1.20.1 where the context is a discussion of perpetual endowments and the words evidently appropriate, in contrast to the case in Pal.192pr.

(ix) *plus* in the sense of 'furthermore' is unique in Pal.188.1.

(x) *praevalere* is found four times in Scaevola, three of them in the LSQPT (twice in Pal.187.1, once in Pal.194). The other is D21.2.69.3.

(xi) *principalis* appears two out of six times in the LSQPT (both times in Pal.193.2) where it means 'principal' referring to an obligation. In three other texts it is used as the adjective from *princeps,* meaning 'imperial': D29.2.98, D32.35pr, D44.7.30. The final example is D49.1.24pr where it designates the 'principal' sum of money as opposed to the interest. But that text is from book 5 of Scaevola's *responsa,* and the *lex geminata* from book 25 of his *digesta* (D42.1.64) lacks the word. Whatever one may think of Schulz's general conclusions from his study of the transmission of these two works of Scaevola, his analyses demonstrated clearly that the *digesta* version represents an earlier stage of the text than that in the *responsa*[31]. This reference to *principalis* therefore lacks authority, but as a (presumably) postclassical insertion is of great interest. We have then no reason to believe that Scaevola ever used the word to mean anything other than 'of or pertaining to the *princeps*'.

Finally, it is worth noting that *principaliter* is found only in Pal.188.1.

(xii) *quid ergo* ...? Only four times in Scaevola, of which three are in the LSQPT: Pal.187.1, 191 and 193.3. The exception is D21.2.69.3.

(xiii) *quid ... retinendum est.* This strange expression is found only in Pal.193.2. It must be translated 'borne in mind, remembered'. Although *retinere* appears in all its forms a further 25 times in Scaevola this sense is never found again.

(xiv) *verius* appears three times in Scaevola, in Pal.187pr and 188.2; and in the strange expression *verius puto* in D47.6.6.1.

Some of these features are quite notable. The following seem of particular interest: firstly, the total absence of some common adverbs from Scaevola's work, yet their appearance in the LSQPT; secondly, the concentration of certain phrases in the LSQPT[32]:

(a) *quid ergo* is found only once outside the LSQPT, but 101 times in Ulpian, 23 in Paul, 7 in Julian, 5 in Pomponius, 4 in Tryphoninus.

(b) Terms concerned with distinction and definition are almost confined to the LSQPT: *differentia, distinguere* and *definire*[33].

(c) *omnimodo.* Three times outside the LSQPT, but 52 in Ulpian, 37 in Paul, 8 in Julian, 20 in Pomponius, and 3 in Tryphoninus.

(d) *verius.* Only once outside the LSQPT, but 108 times in Ulpian, 37 in Paul, 13 in Julian, 10 in Pomponius, 1 in Tryphoninus.

---

[31] *F. Schulz,* 'Überlieferungsgeschichte der *responsa* des Cervidius Scaevola' Symbolae Lenel (Leipzig, 1935) 143-244.

[32] The reasons for selecting these jurists are: Ulpian as representative of the greatest proportion of the Digest; Paul as another major contributor and also as a pupil of Scaevola; Tryphoninus as another pupil of Scaevola; Pomponius as his most likely teacher; Julian owing to his evident importance as a source for the LSQPT.

[33] *F. Pringsheim,* 'Beryt und Bologna' Fs. Lenel (Leipzig, 1921) 204-285 at 220, 235-6, 251- (= Gesammelte Schriften I.391-449 at 402-, 412-3, 424-) argues that these are a preoccupation of the Eastern law schools.

Thirdly, the shift in the meaning of some words is remarkable. This applies particularly to *principalis,* but *retinere* may also be worth noting.

The few remarks on style just made will not cause conviction that the LSQPT differs radically from Scaevola's normal style. That conviction would demand a closer study both of the language of the LSQPT and of Scaevola's style as a whole. Yet it was argued above that linguistic features do not on their own allow judgements as to the authenticity of individual texts. The same must apply to assessing the authenticity of a work. All that a closer study could allow would be a judgement as to whether the LSQPT conforms stylistically to Scaevolan practice. But it would not settle the matter of authenticity.

The last chapter, however, demonstrated with other arguments that large tracts of the LSQPT cannot have been written by Scaevola. So it is not surprising that stylistic differences should also emerge.

3. Three hypotheses

(a) Epitome. The hypothesis that the *liber singularis* is an epitome of Scaevola's twenty-volume work of *quaestiones* has had some support. This was the solution adopted by both *Beseler* and *Schulz* to account for the post-classical elements which they identified in the *liber singularis.* In the absence of a double transmission, however, the relations between the two works cannot be identified with any precision.

A few texts in the *quaestiones* deal with similar problems, but give no firm ground for supposing that the text of the *liber singularis* is derived from the same discussion: (a) Pal.189: a text from book 6 of the *quaestiones,* D35.2.17, discusses the same problem, the making of a will and of codicils, one under military law the other under civil law. The opposite case is discussed (in the *liber singularis* it is the will which is made while a civilian, here it is the codicils).The legal problem is the same; but no more can be said. The same problem is after all discussed by Gaius in a work which there is no reason to believe to be an epitome of Scaevola's *quaestiones.* (b) Pal.190 and 191: D29.2.89 in book 13 deals with abstention by a pupil. (c) Pal.194: D45.1.129 of book 12 discusses disjunctive and alternative obligation. The text is similar to those of Ulpian and Africanus discussed above in chapter II, but there can be no certainty that it is derived from the same context, although Lenel does place it under the edictal rubric E202, *de confessis et indefensis*; D46.1.57 in book 18 deals with suing a *fideiussor.* (d) Pal.187 and 190: D28.3.19 in book 6 deals with problems of substitution.

Similar material can therefore be found in both works of *quaestiones.* This is itself of interest in indicating that the *liber singularis* did not, for example, discuss only problems which were not raised in the twenty-volume work. Nonetheless the opportunities to make connexions between the two works are few and the connexions disappointingly speculative. It is perhaps worth adding three more general reflections.

III. Synthesis

(1) One of the most striking features of the LSQPT is the great formal and substantial disparity between the various fragments. The problems are of varying degrees of difficulty, and of differing character, ranging from a simple enumeration of facts (in Pal.192) to discussion of variations on a casuistic theme (in Pal.188) as well as what looks like more general theorising (Pal.193). Not only is the style and content of the fragments uneven, but there is also no consistency of niveau (Pal.189 and 192 are straightforward; Pal.187 in particular is hard), This cannot be conclusive, but must raise a question over the epitome theory: the epitomator is a purposeful creature with an aim: the original is to be manipulated and condensed in pursuit of that aim. The end result can be expected to show a greater degree of unity than the LSQPT does. At least the general level of treatment should exhibit this, even if content and style do not.

(2) It is relatively uncommon for an epitome to survive together with the original of the work which it epitomises. The motive of the epitomator is to dispose of difficult or out-dated detail. Once this has been done there is no reason (except antiquarianism) to preserve an original of which a more practical version now exists; so the epitome tends to suppress the original[34]. This is of course a generalisation, but nonetheless worth bearing in mind[35].

(3) This relates to the process of excerption. In the Papinian mass the compilers had already excerpted the *libri 20 quaestionum.* In the Appendix mass they then specifically added the LSQPT to the catalogue of works to be excerpted, and the excerpting was carried out by the Papinian committee[36]. This suggests that the LSQPT was not known by the compilers to be an epitome of the *quaestiones* and that it was not easily recognisable as such, in spite of the fact that the compilers had the whole of the works in question whereas we must be content with a small proportion. So (we might argue) either it is not an epitome or it is an epitome so drastic that its origin could easily be overlooked. But how much of an argument it is safe to base on the perceptiveness of the compilers in the last throes of their excerpting it is hard to say[37].

These general arguments; the lack of a double tradition; the complete absence of any positive evidence: all suggest that the hypothesis that the LSQPT is an epitome of the *quaestiones* should be abandoned. It is more difficult to decide between the remaining two possibilities.

---

[34] For some examples, *Wieacker* Textstufen 143-4.

[35] There are shortened versions of some legal works (and others: see *Krueger,* Geschichte 147-8 with nn54 and 55). Gaius' *regulae* are attested in 3 and 1 book versions; Ulpian's in 7 and in 1 (both spurious according to *Honoré,* Ulpian 107-113); Pomponius' enchiridion in 2 and 1. Whether the shorter suppressed the longer in these cases is unclear.

[36] Already argued by Bluhme. *Honoré,* Tribonian 285-6 concurs and assigns the LSQPT to Commissioner F (Cratinus).

[37] The case of Scaevola's *digesta* and *responsa* is quite different: here it is the shorter work (the 6 books of *responsa*) which is found in the Papinian mass, while the longer (40 books of *digesta*) is added in the Appendix: clearly there is a motive to take a larger work subsequently into consideration.

(b) Substantial annotation. The premise is that Scaevola wrote and published a LSQPT. The conception of a textual study on this premise is that the elements which have been added in the course of transmission can be detached by analysis, leaving the original text. It is commonly and plausibly held that the alterations to which a text has been subjected will be in proportion to its practical application[38]; a work employed frequently by practitioners must clearly be updated regularly. It is for this reason that the central works of Ulpian show signs of extensive reworking. Yet, leaving practicality aside, the popularity of a work must also have a bearing on the extent to which its text is subject to interference: a popular work will go through more editions in which changes to the text are bound to occur; little is likely to happen to an abandoned work. In so far it is surprising that there should be so much unclassical material in such a minor work.

If the LSQPT is a genuine work substantially altered, then two main questions have to be faced: (1) the classical origin and nature of the work; (2) the motive and context of the alterations.

(1) This has already been discussed, and the difficulty of accommodating the work in the classical tradition noted.

(2) Since the LSQPT has no apparent practical content, the alterations are hard to explain. Given the style of the work, it seems most likely that it was used in schools, where these alterations must be supposed to have taken place.

The content fails to assist in dating the LSQPT, so the only option is to rely on more general argument. This is inevitably both more speculative and less precise. There are only two broad periods in which the reworking of a classical work can be placed: approximately AD240-300 and AD430-530[39]. The first of these (the so-called 'epiclassical' period[40]) follows directly on the classical period; the second is a time of juristic renaissance in the East. The later of these two periods had a more scholastic character and is thought to have concerned itself more with the preservation than with the re-editing of classical texts: serious alterations are unlikely to have been made at that time[41]. So if the unclassical elements in the LSQPT are regarded as alterations to an original text, they are principally to be placed in the second half of the third century.

But substantial unclassical elements have been detected, which amount to about a third of the extant work. This causes a difficulty, if we suppose that roughly the same proportion was added throughout the work. For the work is a *liber singularis*. It occupied one roll of papyrus. Yet how could an extra third be added to Scaevola's text and the whole still contained in one roll? And if it was no

---

[38] *Wieacker*, Textstufen 175-7.
[39] ibid.
[40] *Wieacker*, RHD 49 (1971) 223.
[41] *Wieacker*, Textstufen 177.

longer contained in one roll how could it still be referred to as a *liber singularis*[42]? The solution to this problem is to suppose that the additions were made to the LSQPT when it was already in *codex* form. However long (within reason) the *codex*, it could still be described as a *liber singularis*. It is around AD240 that juristic works seem to have begun to be transcribed from roll into *codex*[43]. Since this process naturally began with practical reference works[44], it does not seem likely that the LSQPT would have been dealt with very early. This argument would supply a terminus post quem for the alterations of around AD260-270.

(c) Wholly spurious? The premise here is that Scaevola did not write and publish a LSQPT. Textual study on this premise aims to reveal the sources from which the work is composed and to account for its attribution. That this hypothesis is not much more drastic than the previous one has already been pointed out, but is on the other hand not to be assumed without strong support. Spurious juristic works have been identified before. The radical textual criticism of the early part of this century was too swift perhaps to condemn, but some of its conclusions have found support after more judicious investigations. *Libri singulares* in particular have been the target of much attack, especially the serried ranks (sixty one) of those attributed to Paul[45]. The considerable difference, however, in the volume of those attributed to Paul and those to Scaevola (two) means that generalisations from Paul are out of place. Even in Paul's case there is no doubt that some works have been dismissed too hastily[46], and that a presumption of inauthenticity against all is methodologically unsound[47].

All the same, the chances in antiquity of passing off my book as Scaevola's were by no means unfavourable. Quintilian in the preface to his work says that his decision to publish it was encouraged *eo magis quod duo iam sub nomine meo libri ferebantur artis rhetoricae neque editi a me neque in hoc comparati*[48]. Similarly the tally of Galen's writings made the forger's task easier and prompted Galen to publish a book *de libris propriis* which catalogued the authentic[49]. The same circumstances need not of course apply to law as do to rhetoric or medicine, but

---

[42] But we cannot be sure that this was the classical title. In some cases numbers of books (or the qualification *singularis*) seem to have been added for description only later: cf. the unqualified *responsorum liber* of Julius Aquila, with *D. Liebs,* ANRW II.15 (1976) 357.

[43] *Wieacker,* Textstufen 103.

[44] ibid. 98.

[45] *A. Guarino,* Adfinitas (Milan, 1939) 97n15; *Gaudemet,* Formation 86-7.

[46] For example Paul's *liber singularis de iuris et facti ignorantia,* the subject of an attack by *F. Ebrard,* SZ 45 (1925) 118.

[47] So *D. Liebs,* Die Klagenkonkurrenz im röm. Recht (Göttingen, 1972) 167- with a clear and comprehensive survey of *libri singulares.*

[48] Quintilian *inst. or.* pr. 7; cf. *W. Speyer,* Die literarische Fälschung im heidnischen und christlichen Altertum (Munich, 1971) 40.

[49] Cf. *G. Bowersock* in Cambridge History of Classical Literature I (Greek literature) edd. P. Easterling and B.M.W.Knox (Cambridge, 1985) 662; *Speyer,* Fälschung 120, 123 (with a few more examples).

3. Three hypotheses

Galen was a contemporary of Scaevola and his experience is valuable testimony to the conditions prevailing at the time. Quintilian and Galen both refer to forgeries of their own works during their lifetimes. But to pass off a work once the ostensible author has died is a simpler matter, since he is no longer on hand to dispense an unchallengeable judgement on the imputed authorship. So the forger's practical difficulties should not be exaggerated.

For a juristic work the motive of a false attribution is presumably to acquire a greater authority for a work when cited in court. This is *Honoré's* explanation of the spurious works attributed to Ulpian[50]. Another possibility is that it was a commercial ploy to increase sales[51]. The temptation to attribute a work to a famous name was no doubt great—even if the risks of its being unmasked as a forgery were proportionally greater[52]. But if the LSQPT is spurious, the question of attribution remains to be resolved. Most postclassical compilations are naturally enough attributed to Ulpian or Paul.

As for dating the composition of a spurious LSQPT, the best approach is to consider what postclassical works it resembles. Such works tend to be short and devoid of argumentation[53], although it is true that they show little uniformity. Hermogenian's work for example builds principally on classical casuistic literature, and so belongs to the higher, more ambitious reaches of postclassical work[54], while the (only slightly later) *collatio* has altogether more humble aims. The works spuriously attributed to Ulpian are believed to stem from the period before AD 300[55]; some doubtful *libri singulares* appear to originate in it[56]: as a candidate for the origin of the LSQPT it is perhaps the most plausible. The classicism of the LSQPT (references, for instance, in Pal.193 to the formulary system) would also support a dating in the reign of Diocletian. *Beseler* thought the LSQPT bore much the same relation to Scaevola's *quaestiones* as the fifth-century Autun paraphrase of Gaius does to the real Gaius[57]. Since there is little reason to believe that the LSQPT is an epitome or paraphrase of the *quaestiones*, this comparison is misleading. Not in content but in niveau the LSQPT bears some resemblance to the *fragmenta Vaticana* (of more or less AD 300): both contain unclassical elements which are mostly not of a practical nature but demonstrate misunderstanding of classical law[58]. Some problems however (notably Pal.187.1 and 191) are evidently based on casuistic treatment in classical

---

[50] *Honoré*, Ulpian 128.
[51] Cf. *D. Liebs*, Romanitas-Christianitas (ed. G. Wirth: Berlin, 1982) 292.
[52] Quintilian *inst. or.* 1.8.21: these considerations led to a flood of works by non-existent authors.
[53] *D. Liebs*, Studi Volterra 5 (Milan, 1971) 63.
[54] *D. Liebs*, Hermogenians iuris epitomae (Göttingen, 1964) 88.
[55] *Honoré*, Ulpian 128 (except for the *libri opinionum*).
[56] *Wieacker*, RHD 49 (1971) 217-.
[57] *Beseler*, SZ 44 (1924) 359.
[58] *Wieacker*, SZ 67 (1950) 397.

literature (especially in Julian); in this respect the LSQPT belongs in the higher postclassical reaches together with Hermogenian's epitome (of c.AD302-315). That, interestingly enough, also uses Julian as a source[59].

But was a text of Julian used directly? Or was the only access to him through citation in the Severan commentaries? Caution is required here, and it has sometimes been found wanting[60]; but after careful consideration *Liebs* is prepared to suggest that Hermogenian may have had direct access to Julian[61]. For any later period direct use of Julian is certainly out of the question, for Julian was not among the top five in the law of citations[62], and his absence from that law makes it highly unlikely that his work was available in the fifth century (the only other serious possibility for dating) to be quarried for the LSQPT[63].

These arguments for dating the work before AD300, the period of Hermogenian and of classicism, are not irresistible but seem persuasive.

---

[59] *Liebs*, Hermogenian 78.

[60] R. *Taubenschlag*, Opera minora I (Warsaw, 1959) 7n31 thought that Diocletian's chancellery had direct access to Julian's *digesta*. But as *Liebs* ibid. 87n273 points out, he gives only one example which is a citation of Julian in a text of Ulpian and so does not prove the availability of Julian's work.

[61] *Liebs*, ibid. 78-9; cf. *Wieacker*, Textstufen 174.

[62] C.Th. 1.4.3 (426).

[63] The *interpretatio* (written soon after AD450) to the law of citations says that the works of Julian, like other high classical works, were no longer extant: *Scaevola Sabinus Julianus atque Marcellus in suis corporibus non inveniuntur*.

IV. Conclusions

Three hypotheses have been put forward. In the last chapter only one was rejected: that the LSQPT is an epitome of the *quaestiones*. In the interest of reaching as judicious a conclusion as possible, both the strengths and the weaknesses of the other two hypotheses have been put forward. But it is time to reject another: the second. In my view it is the third and last hypothesis which is most plausible: Scaevola did not write a *liber singularis quaestionum publice tractatarum*. The last chapter attempted to show that the hypothesis that Scaevola did not write it, but that it was composed from classical elements combined with postclassical, is hardly more extreme than the hypothesis that the work was genuinely published by Scaevola but in its extant form contains approximately one third of postclassical material.

Sources and genre are the two elements which are most persuasive in this verdict. The works of classical jurisprudence can be divided into genres with astonishing neatness, but the impossibility of assigning the LSQPT to one suggests that it is out of place in the classical period. The structure of some of the surviving fragments also speaks for more than annotation, however substantial, since the extensive unclassical material is not always readily separable from material which could be classical.

As for sources, there is a close but rather ambivalent relationship with Julian which seems to stretch from a tendency to select arguments discussed by him, through glossing from discussions in his works, to full-scale reworking of his texts. It cannot be shown conclusively that the texts which are just parallel to Julian must have been taken from his work by a postclassical writer. Some of those texts contain argument which is classically sound; and there are also texts which seem sound but for which no parallel in Julian can be found. What is their origin? It is not necessary to suppose that it must be Scaevola, since if the LSQPT (or any other work) is identified as spurious then to opt for the compromise of presuming that it was derived from the works of the ostensible author is to exaggerate the scruples of the compiler.

The situation is this: the postclassical compiler used classical sources, some of which can be associated with Julian; others can not; he also contributed material himself. The most economical hypothesis is that the source of all the classical matter is Julian, but owing to the vagaries of transmission through the Digest commission we cannot demonstrate this for all surviving fragments. But here we stumble against the difficulty of attribution. If the work was really a compilation from Julian, it would plainly be more natural to attribute it to him, a jurist with a reputation greater than Scaevola's. In these circumstances an attribution to Scaevola is inconceivable. How might it be explained?

(1) What about another Scaevola? It was perhaps to Mucius Scaevola that the postclassical compiler attributed his work, intending not a false attribution but a reference to one of the fathers of Roman jurisprudence. The law of citations mentions a Scaevola, but it is not clear to which it is referring[1]. The list appears however to be in chronological order, and the name Scaevola precedes Sabinus. It seems that Mucius must have been intended. His repute lasted perhaps even longer, and his name conjured up venerable traditions of Roman jurisprudence. Mucius Scaevola had evidently become proverbial, for in a letter Symmachus writes of the *eruditio Scaevolarum*; it cannot have been to Cervidius that he was referring[2]. If this is right, then the postclassical teacher who pillaged the classics for his textbook had a keen sense of tradition.

(2) The same Scaevola? Cervidius Scaevola was also a well-known jurist, praised with Paul and Ulpian by Modestinus[3], described by Arcadius and Honorius as the *auctor prudentissimus iurisconsultorum*[4]. So his reputation lasted through the fourth century. To judge from his extant writings, Cervidius was a specialist in matters of succession, with which almost the whole of the LSQPT is concerned. A well-known and appropriate name, then, but still hardly one to oust Julian and to be the object of a wholly fanciful attribution.

Neither of these suggestions could be described as enticing, let alone irresistible. If both the first thesis (of mistaken identity) and the second (a completely fanciful attribution to Cervidius Scaevola) are rejected, then in order to account for the attribution we are forced to the conclusion that Scaevolan elements were employed in the compilation of the LSQPT. It is they that must be the sound classical elements for which no parallel has been found. So the LSQPT was not written and published by Scaevola, but the attribution to him is based on the genuine use of his works as one of the sources.

Where might these Scaevolan elements come from? We can only speculate. Parallels in the extant works are too few and too weak to be convincing. The cases in the LSQPT can only come from works not extant. That is not a problem, for the Digest commission was supposed to dispose of any duplication; and although it did not succeed in this objective entirely, it might have kept it up for the compass of one *liber*. Or else the cases in the LSQPT may be unpublished problems discussed by Scaevola. Here there is the difficulty of accounting for

---

[1] C.Th. 1.4.3: *Conrat*, Mél. Fitting I (1907) 320 and *Wieacker*, Textstufen 158 both take the text to refer to Mucius Scaevola; *Krueger*, Geschichte 299n17 suggests that there is a confusion of both Scaevolae.

[2] Symmachus *ep.* 3.23.

[3] Mod. D27.1.13.2 lib 4 excusationum.

[4] C.Th. 4.4.3.3 (396).

IV. Conclusions

someone having access to Scaevola's unpublished work. All the same, the title of the LSQPT may suggest an origin in teaching: books entitled *quaestiones* appear to have originated not in the course of practical work but in teaching, in the *disputatio fori*[5]. Some have attempted to explain the *publice* of the title of the LSQPT in relation to this, supposing *disputatio* to be tuition confined to one's own pupils, but public disputation to be partly accessible to a wider public[6]. And it is perhaps tempting to make a link with the reference to *publicae disputationes* in a constitution of Diocletian[7], precisely the period after all in which the LSQPT is to be dated.

So there are three strands in the LSQPT: cases taken from Scaevola; contributions from other classical works, particularly from the *digesta* of Julian; the postclassical arguments and theorising. The LSQPT is a postclassical compilation. Starting, no doubt, with some texts of Scaevola, the compiler proceeded to compile. He wrote a bit himself, and borrowed not a little from Julian. This is the explanation of the long passages of evidently unclassical theorising. And it accounts too for the frequent reminiscences of Julian, for the compiler naturally enough reflected his own reading in his compilation.

To what readership might he have aspired? It does not seem to be possible to connect the LSQPT with what is known about the eastern postclassical law schools. It is tempting, of course, to try to link it with the *liber singularis de testamentis*, one of the *libri singulares* used in postclassical legal education[8]. Views on these *libri singulares* differ, particularly on the question whether they are based on or extracted from Ulpian's *libri ad Sabinum*[9], or are 'anonymous postclassical compositions'[10]. But it is accepted that the first year of postclassical education was concerned with civil (as opposed to edictal) matters, and so with Sabinian material. Unfortunately the LSQPT does not fit this scheme very well. Although four fragments (Pal.187 to 190) fit neatly into the topics which would

---

[5] *Krueger,* Geschichte 145 whose view is that the cases are mostly not practical; for another view, *Liebs,* ANRW II.15 (1976) 205n47.

[6] *Krueger,* ibid. 151 with n75; *Liebs,* ibid. 220n131. But the suggestion of *Liebs* in Studi Volterra 5 (1971) 60n41 (61) that Marci. D20.3.1.2 refers to Scaevola's *variae quaestiones* in order to distinguish the *quaestiones* from the LSQPT is not plausible. Distinguishing must have been easy: confusion could after all arise only when speaking of book 1 of the *quaestiones;* and Marcian is speaking of book 3.

[7] Diocl. C9.41.11.1 (290).

[8] C. Omnem 1.

[9] *Krueger,* Geschichte 395-6. For a detailed discussion of this view, *Wieacker,* Textstufen 133-.

[10] *Schulz,* History 275 (= Geschichte 351). But *Schulz* has little evidence for his view and cites only his own argument in TR 17 (1941) 19-27 that P. Ryl. 479 is not a Digest manuscript but a manuscript of an earlier compilation. Yet the differences between the Digest and the papyrus texts are extremely slight, and it is easier to believe *R. Düll* and *E. Seidl,* SZ 61 (1941) 406-410, who attribute the discrepancies to the poor quality of the papyrus text. The papyrus is in any case composed of fragments expressly attributed to various authors, so is quite a different matter from the LSQPT.

be covered (institution of heirs, slaves, pupils; the military will; acquisition and failure to acquire inheritance), the others are less promising: Pal.193 is Sabinian but deals with the wrong subject (obligations); Pal.186 is concerned with the *lex Iulia de maritandis ordinibus*; Pal.192 (an interdict) and 194 (a praetorian promise) are plainly edictal, and so is probably Pal.191, whether one chooses to regard as its main issue abstention by a pupil, fraud or *in integrum restitutio*. The LSQPT cannot then be one of the four *libri singulares* mentioned by Justinian as part of the educational programme at the eastern law schools in the fifth century.

Yet the LSQPT is in any case to be dated much earlier than the fifth century; and, although this is far from settled, there seem to be a few hints that it is of western origin. In the LSQPT there is much discussion of complex cases, and some familiarity with classical concepts (albeit coupled with lamentable misunderstandings) is shown. These facts mean that the work cannot be dated later than AD300. Its compiler's acquaintance with Julian confirms this.

The style of the LSQPT is right for the schools. It is true that in some respects it seems unsatisfactory as a school text: there is a great variation in difficulty between individual fragments, which would present problems not just for classical but also for postclassical students. Some of it would have been too easy and some much too complex. This does not mean, however, that it cannot have been a textbook; simply that it cannot have been a good textbook. As for the contents, it does not seem to be simply a textbook on the law of succession, since other topics are treated too, if not very thoroughly. But in spite of this failure to delimit its material and maintain a uniform level, the LSQPT has a very pronounced academic character. The arguments are painstaking; there is a fondness for rhetorical contrasts and distinctions; attempts to extract general rules and definitions are an obsession. The classicising elements also fit this pattern. So do the cases discussed, which are far from practical and have a hypothetical and scholastic character.

Style and contents and the sources employed show that the LSQPT is to be dated before AD300, and located in the schools. There are a few hints of western promise. So it is most likely that the work originates in the law school at Rome. A blank canvas would capture all the lively detail of our knowledge of the law schools and their syllabus earlier than the fifth century and in the West. But the LSQPT allows us to discern a few lines representing the character of teaching material, and depicting the level of legal culture and competence. Restoration of the colours may take rather longer.

Index of sources

1. Non-legal

Apuleius, *Apologia*
36   11 n.4

Aulus Gellius *Noctes Atticae*
praefatio   11 n.8, 13 n.16
3.9.1   11 n.7
6.10.2   11 n.5
7.5.1   11 n.8
14.8.2   11 n.5
16.8.14   75 n.217, n.218

Libanius *orationes*
2.44   86 n.16
48.22   86 n.16
62.21-23   86 n.16

Pliny *epistulae*
1.20.1   5

Quintilian *institutio oratoria*
1 pr.7   94 n.48
1.8.21   95 n.52

Symmachus *epistulae*
3.23   98 n.2
P. Ryl. 474   86 n.16
479   99 n.10

2. Legal

Gaius *Institutiones*
2.64   64 n.183
2.174   15 n.10, 21 n.33
2.176   21 n.33
2.182   35 n.76
2.185-8   18 n.21
2.187   19
2.195   19 n.26
2.196   19 n.24
2.271   34 n.73
3.79   58 n.154
3.120   77 n.223
4.91   71 n.205
4.101   71 n.205, 77 n.222
4.119   68 n.197
4.151   61 n.166

Paul *sententiae*
3.4b.7   19 n.29
5.9.4   70 n.201

Paul *sententiae: interpretatio*
5.10.4   70 n.201

Ulpian *epitome*
22.12   18 n.21

Codex Theodosianus
1.4.3.   96 n.62, 98 n.1
4.4.3.3   98 n.4

Codex Theodosianus: interpretatio
4.2.1   70 n.201
5.1.5   70 n.201

Appendix Visigothorum
1.3   70 n.201

Basilica
35.10.45   18 n.20

Corpus Iuris Civilis
C Omnem 1   99 n.8

Institutiones
2.14pr   18 n.21
2.20.34   29 n.59
4.15.4a   62 n.172

Codex
3.32.3   64 n.181
6.23.24   29 n.59, 34 n.73
6.27.5   20, 29, 31 n.62
6.37.24   34 n.73
6.38.4   75 n.218
7.43.8   78 n.227
9.41.11   12 n.9, 99 n.7

Digesta
1.1.10pr   59 n.157
4.4.31   53

Index of sources

7.1.12.2	28 n.54	29.3.11	31 n.64, 35 n.77, 41 n.103
7.1.13.2	67 n.193	29.7.2.2	41
7.1.25.6	16 n.15	29.7.8.4	42 n.105
8.5.20.1	62 n.174	29.7.9.1	42 n.105
11.7.46pr	49 n.129	29.7.14pr	41
12.6.61	52 f.	29.7.20.1	42 n.105
13.1.18	89	29.7.25	42 n.105
13.7.8.3	64 n.183	30.81.1	15
15.1.51	89, 90	30.81.10	31 n.64
16.1.13.2	67 n.193	30.94pr	37 n.84, 83 n.4
17.2.25	28	30.126pr	34 n.73, 36 f., 38 n.89, 39 n.94
17.2.26	28	31.14pr	26
18.1.26	51 n.136	31.20	16 n.13
20.3.1.2	99 n.6	31.27	74 n.215
20.4.21.1	89	31.89.4	64 n.183
21.2.69.3	90	32.1.6	37 n.83
23.3.7.3	65 n.185	32.6.1	35 n.75, 37 n.83
24.3.64.10	14	32.35pr	90
24.3.65	14, 80 ff.	32.37.2	90
27.1.13.2	98 n.3	32.103pr-1	32 ff., 80 ff.
28.2.29.6	89	32.103.2-3	37 ff., 80 ff.
28.3.19	91	33.1.20.1	63 n.174, 90
28.5.50pr	19 n.29	33.2.38pr	89
28.5.55	31 f., 83	33.7.27.2	28 n.55
28.6.2.2	83 n.4	34.1.16.1	89
28.6.2.4	31 n.63, 35 n.77	34.4.30.4	90
28.6.10.7	20 f., 83	34.5.13.2	12 n.13
28.6.16pr	31 n.64	35.2.11.5	35 n.74, n.77
28.6.18.1	31 n.63	35.2.11.8	34
28.6.34.2	38 n.87	35.2.17	42 n.106, 91
28.6.35	38 n.88, n.89, 39 f., 83	35.2.57	28
28.6.48pr	14 ff., 80 ff.	35.2.60	35 n.73
28.6.48.1	17 ff., 80 ff.	35.2.87.4-5	38 n.93, 40 n.96
28.6.48.2	30 ff., 80 ff.	35.2.87.7-8	33 f., 40 n.96, 83
28.8.5.1	56 n.150	35.2.96	40 f., 80 ff.
28.8.7pr	51 n.136	36.1.3.1	41 n.101
28.8.7.3	51 n.136, 56 n.150	36.1.6.2	43 n.109
29.1.17.1	43 n.112, 44 n.113	36.1.28.3-4	43 n.109, 83 n.4
29.1.17.4	42	36.1.61pr	70 n.201
29.1.18	42 n.196	36.1.69.2	44 n.113
29.1.20pr	42 n.196	36.1.81	43 ff., 80 ff.
29.2.38	43 n.112	36.1.82	70 n.201
29.2.42pr	36 n.79	36.2.7.4	35 n.78
29.2.44	50, 53, 83 n.4	37.4.3.11	67 n.193
29.2.53.1	43 n.112	37.4.10.4	67 n.193
29.2.55	43 n.112	37.5.1pr	37 n.86
29.2.56	43 n.112	37.5.5pr-1	38 n.89, 39 n.94
29.2.57pr	43 n.109, 50 n.133	37.5.5.5	39 n.94
29.2.64	16	37.5.5.8	39 n.94
29.2.65	17	37.10.7.5	43 n.112, 44 n.113
29.2.67	15	37.11.2.4	21 n.33
29.2.68	15 n.10	37.11.2.8	15 n.11
29.2.71.3-4	54	40.4.10.1	26
29.2.71.8	55 n.147	40.5.50	25
29.2.71.9	54	40.7.2.1-2	31 n.64
29.2.89	91	40.7.2.4	31
29.2.98	90	40.7.28.1	28 n.54
29.2.99	43 n.112	40.7.36	31 n.62

Index of sources

41.1.23.3	15 n.16	46.1.21.2	67 n.195, 69 n.199, 83
41.2.3.23	58 n.154	46.1.21.4	70 n.201
41.2.13.2	65 n.185, n.186	46.1.50	67 n.194, 69 n.198
41.2.13.6-11	61 n.167, 65 n.185	46.1.57	91
42.1.64	90	46.1.63	64 n.183
42.4.7.10	45 n.116	46.1.71pr	70 n.201
42.4.8	56 n.150	46.2.8.3	71 n.206
42.5.6pr	44 n.113	46.3.78	28 n.54
42.5.6.1	51	46.3.93	65 ff., 80 ff.
42.5.6.2	49, 53, 56, 83	46.3.95.2-3	67 n.194, 70 n.201
42.5.28	31 n.64, 35 n.77, 36 n.79	46.3.107	69 n.198
42.6.3pr	67 n.195, n.196	46.4.20	73 n.213
42.8.6.7	57 f., 83	46.7.4	72 n.211, 83
42.8.10.10	53 n.141	46.7.5.2	73 f.
42.8.10.16	57 f.	46.7.6	73 n.213
42.8.24	47 ff., 80 ff.	46.7.10	77 n.222
44.3.6.1	65 n.188	46.7.13pr	74 ff.
44.3.14	60 ff., 80 ff.	46.7.14	72 n.211, 83
44.3.16	65 n.188	46.7.21	70 ff., 80 ff.
44.4.4.27	65 n.186	47.2.74	64 n.183
44.7.30	90	47.6.6.1	90
45.1.63	74 n.215, 83	48.10.14.2	14 n.3
45.1.129	74 n.215, 91	49.1.24pr	90
45.2.13	66 f.	49.14.29.2	70 n.201
45.3.19	16 n.15	50.16.124	75 n.217
46.1.5	67 f., 69 n.200, 83	50.17.202	62 n.169
46.1.14	67 n.195		

Printed by Libri Plureos GmbH
in Hamburg, Germany